RUNNING LINUX

COMPANION CD-ROM

INSTALLATION GUIDE

RUNNING LINUX COMPANION CD-ROM

INSTALLATION GUIDE

MARC EWING

O'REILLY & ASSOCIATES, INC.
103 MORRIS STREET, SUITE A
SEBASTOPOL, CA 95472

Running Linux Companion CD-ROM Installation Guide

by Marc Ewing

Editor: Andy Oram

Production Editor: Clairemarie Fisher O'Leary

Printing History:

January 1996: First Edition.

This book is printed on acid-free paper with 85% recycled content, 15% post-consumer waste. O'Reilly & Associates is committed to using paper with the highest recycled content available consistent with high quality.

Table of Contents

CHAPTER FOUR

CHAPTER FIVE

CHAPTER SIX

CHAPTER SEVEN

Preface

The two CD–ROMs in this package contain a complete computing environment for your enjoyment. In addition to the basic Linux operating system for Intel platforms, the disks have XFree86 for a graphical interface, a wealth of utilities, and complete source code for their contents. This is a full Linux distribution, called Red Hat Linux.

Red Hat Software, Inc. has collaborated with O'Reilly & Associates to put together this book/CD–ROM package. Red Hat assembled all the software, created the installation procedures, and wrote the installation booklet, which O'Reilly & Associates edited. Red Hat and O'Reilly & Associates will update this package regularly with stable versions of the Red Hat Linux, so you can obtain updates cheaply and easily.

This book gives basic information on installation. For details about making full use of your system, you'll also want to buy *Running Linux* by Matt Welsh and Lar Kaufman. That is why we called this package a "Companion CD–ROM"—it's not meant to be used in isolation. *Running Linux* offers a background in Linux system administration that you'll want to have in order to configure your system the way you need it. Its installation information also may help you out of a jam, particularly when you are configuring the X Window System. The book tells you how to set up basic networking and a Web server. Finally, it offers a wealth of introductory material on things you can *do* with your new system.

Advantages of Red Hat Linux

Linux, like UNIX itself, is a very modular operating system. The skills required to select, compile, link, and install the various components needed for a complete Linux are beyond the experience of most people who might want to use Linux. The various Linux distributions go a long way towards solving this for the average

Linux user, but most do not address the problem of how to upgrade your Linux system once you get it successfully installed. Most users found it easier to delete their whole Linux system and reinstall from scratch when they needed to upgrade.

The Red Hat distribution makes Linux easier to install and maintain by providing the user with advanced package management, graphical (point and click) system installation and control, and system administration tools. Red Hat clearly separates the files that are required for each piece of software you're interested in and puts them in packages. You can install or remove each package without worrying about the effect that has on the rest of the system. The packaging system, called Red Hat Package Manager (RPM), is discussed in Chapter 7, *Control-Panel*.

In a short time, Red Hat Linux has become widely accepted and has many users. It seems that most everyone who gives Red Hat a chance has found it superior to all other Linux distributions they've tried.

How to Use This Book

On most systems, Red Hat Linux is easy to install: the installation script can walk you through the process in as little as 15 minutes. The installation system is very flexible: you can install and uninstall individual software "packages" with a couple of clicks of your mouse button. It is easy to maintain: package installations can be verified and corrected. Finally, it is easy to administer: a set of graphical administration tools bundled into a "control–panel" reduce the hassle of every day system administration.

If you are knowledgeable about Linux and are itching to install Red Hat Linux right away, check out Chapter 2, *Quick Start*. After reading that you should be able to do a basic installation without much trouble. For new Linux users, we would suggest reading through the entire manual first to get a good understanding of the various systems and installation procedures.

Acknowledgments

We would like to thank Linus Torvalds and the hundreds of developers around the world for creating, truly, one of the wonders of distributed development.

At Red Hat Software, Donnie Barnes, Marc Ewing, and Erik Troan co–wrote this book. At O'Reilly & Associates, Andy Oram reviewed and edited the installation booklet, and passed his comments back to Red Hat so they could be incorporated into the free version of the document. Lorrie LeJeune served as product manager and advocate.

Also at O'Reilly & Associates, Clairemarie Fisher O'Leary copyedited and guided the book through the production process, Kismet McDonough provided quality checking, and Lenny Muellner and Erik Ray provided tools support. The cover was designed by Edie Freedman, with modifications by Hanna Dyer. Hanna also worked on the development of the package design.

CHAPTER ONE

Hardware Requirements

All devices that have drivers in the standard Linux kernel are supported in the Red Hat kernel, except sound cards. The reason there is no direct sound support is that there is no way to build all the sound drivers into one kernel. The sound drivers also require important parameters to be configured at compile time. For these two reasons, we felt that we should just leave sound support out at this time. You can, however, compile your own kernel with sound support after installation. For more information on how to do this, see the Kernel–HOWTO (which would be in */usr/doc/HOWTO*).

For more information on special hardware that is supported by the kernel directly, including SCSI devices, see the Hardware–HOWTO and the SCSI–HOWTO (also in */usr/doc/HOWTO*). There is an XFree86 HOWTO as well that lists video cards that are supported.

There is no ftape support in the standard Red Hat kernels. This means that you have to recompile your kernel in order to use a QIC–40, QIC–80, QIC–117, or other floppy–controller based tape devices.

All installs require a 1.44M floppy drive connected as the first physical floppy device (`a:`). Here are the requirements for various popular combinations of software:

Minimum Text-based Installation

- 386sx or better CPU
- 8M RAM

- 40M hard drive
- Any working video card (Hercules, CGA, VGA, SVGA, etc.)
- Any supported CD–ROM drive

Minimum Text-based Installation, with X Window System

- 386sx or better CPU
- 8M RAM
- 80M hard drive
- Any XFree86 supported video card (VGA, and SVGA, see below)
- Mouse (most types are supported)
- Any supported CD–ROM drive

Minimum X-based Installation

- 386sx or better CPU
- 12M RAM
- 80M hard drive
- Any XFree86 supported video card (VGA, and SVGA, see below)
- Mouse (most types are supported)
- Any supported CD–ROM drive

Recommended Configuration

- 486dx or better CPU
- 16M RAM
- 300M hard drive
- Any XFree86 supported SVGA card
- 3 button mouse
- SCSI tape drive (optional)
- UPS (optional)
- Double spin CD–ROM drive

Supported video cards include:

- Most diamond cards
- Most S3 based cards

- ET4000 based cards
- ATI cards
- Cirrus Logic 542x and 543x
- Chips and Technologies based cards
- Trident 8900 and 9400
- Most #9 cards

Cards that are unsupported right now include Matrox cards and the Trident 9440 based cards.

Supported CD–ROM drives include:

- All IDE/ATAPI compliant drives
- All SCSI drives connected to a *supported* controller card
- All sound blaster interface drives (the Matsushta/Kotobuki/Panasonic one)
- Mitsumi drives
- Sony 535, CDU 31, CDU 33

CHAPTER TWO

Quick Start

This chapter tells you how to install Red Hat Linux if you are already experienced at Linux installations. If you don't understand this chapter, read the following one, which goes into much more detail.

Make a Boot Disk and Ramdisks

When you boot the Linux kernel during installation, it prompts you to insert a "ramdisk." A better term is "root disk," but we'll stick to "ramdisk" as long as that term appears in the kernel messages.

Check the *README* file on the CD–ROM. It contains the latest information on your release, some of which may be different from what you are about to read.

The *images* directory is the root of the boot disk images. Look at the file *version.idx* and choose a kernel version. Change to the proper kernel version directory. Read the *image.txt* file and choose a hardware configuration. Choose the boot image *bootXXXX.img* that corresponds to the image listed in the file. Use *dd* or *rawrite.exe* (found in the *dosutils* directory) to write the proper boot image file to a formatted high density (1.44Mb) 3.5 inch floppy.

Do the same for the two ramdisks, using the *images/ramdisk1.img* and *images/ramdisk2.img* images.

If you are creating these disks from an existing Linux system, just run *mkfloppies.pl* which will help you create your floppies.

Install

Insert the boot floppy into drive A, and insert the CD–ROM into your CD–ROM drive (for a CD–ROM install) or connect to your network (for an FTP or NFS install). Then reboot, insert the ramdisks disk when asked, and answer all questions as they are presented.

Running Directly Off the CD-ROM

If your Red Hat Linux CD–ROM came with a "live filesystem" you can run (with some limitations) Red Hat right off the CD–ROM without installing anything on your hard drive. This can be useful if you just wish to try out Red Hat or have a look at the graphical system administration tools. It can also be used as a learning environment for new Linux users, allowing them to get familiar with the environment and new commands without going through a complete installation.

If there is a README file on your Live Filesystem CD–ROM, read it. It contains the latest information on your CD–ROM, some of which may be different from what you are about to read.

First, you need to create boot and ramdisks. The *images* directory on the CD–ROM contains all the disk images. For an explanation of how to select and create the proper boot disk for your hardware, see the section called "Creating Boot and Root Disks" in Chapter 3, *Installation in Detail.* The ramdisk image is *liveram.img.* Use *dd* or *rawrite* to write *liveram.img* to your second floppy disk.

If you'd like to store some files between sessions, you may create a disk for */home* by following the instructions at boot time. Be sure to have a blank floppy ready.

Now boot your system with the boot floppy (with the CD–ROM inserted), and insert the ramdisk when prompted. The system will probe for your CD–ROM. If it does not find it you will need to reboot and enter parameters at the `LILO boot:` prompt to force detection of your CD–ROM drive. See the section called "Booting the Installation System" in Chapter 3 for more details.

If you are going to use a */home* floppy disk, insert it now. If it isn't already formatted, it will be formatted before being mounted at */home.* While using the system, you can copy files to */home* to save them.

If you are not using a */home* floppy, type `n` and press Enter.

When the login prompt appears log in as `root`. To run the X Window System (which you'll want to do so you can try the control panel and glint) first run *Xconfigurator* to configure X for your hardware. The *Xconfigurator* and its use are described in the section called "X Window System Configuration" in Chapter 4, *Post-Installation Configuration.* To start X, enter *startx.* You can now hack around to your heart's content!

To stop X, type Control–Alt–Backspace. To shutdown the system, type *shutdown –h now.*

CHAPTER THREE

INSTALLATION IN DETAIL

Most people find Red Hat Linux installation to be painless. If all your hardware is configured properly, is compatible with Linux, and can be recognized by Linux at boot time, rest assured that the hard part is done.

Although you will be doing your first installation off of the CD–ROMs included with this book, you may want to get new kernels from the Red Hat FTP site for upgrades, particularly unstable intermediate kernels for which we will not publish new versions of this Companion CD–ROM. For that reason, we are including directions for an installation via FTP.

Furthermore, if you have a network of machines (even non–Linux machines) linked together by the Network File System (NFS), you can put the CD–ROMs on a drive mounted on one machine and then load the software onto other systems over NFS. Directions for this procedure are also included here.

Before You Begin

If Linux will coexist on your machine with OS/2, you will need to create your partitions with the OS/2 partitioning software. This is very important. During the installation, do not create any new partitions, but do set the partition types properly for the Linux partitions.

If you will be connected to a network, be sure you know your IP address, network address, net mask, broadcast address, gateway IP address, and name server IP addresses. If you don't know these values, ask your network administrator for them.

You will need three formatted 3.5 inch high density (1.44Mb) floppy disks for boot disk and ramdisks to be used for installation. You may want to have a fourth disk to create a recovery ramdisk for your final system. This is highly recommended as it allows you to recover from filesystem corruption and other mishaps.

Read all of the installation instructions before starting the installation. By doing so you will be prepared for any decisions that need to be made and won't have any surprises.

Starting the Installation

The installation instructions in this chapter are divided into three sections. This section applies to all installations. After finishing this section, you should continue with the section called "Graphical Installation" for X–based installations, or with the section called "Continuing a Text Installation" for text–based installations (including floppy and FTP installations).

Creating Boot and Root Disks

You must first create a boot disk and two ramdisks to use during the installation. These must be 1.44 Mb 3.5 inch floppies. The disk images for these disks are located under the *images* directory.

After changing to the *images* directory, change to the proper kernel version directory. In most cases, there will only be one kernel version. Its directory will be the version number with the periods removed (i.e., kernel 1.2.13 will be in directory *1213*). Read the file *image.txt* and choose a hardware configuration. The only ambiguity here is the fact that there is an "Other" category of ethernet cards. This is the category that the NE–2000 and many other cards are in. If your card is supported under Linux and is not listed elsewhere, it should be in this category.

Please note that all images have support for ATAPI CD–ROM drives, and that a SCSI CD–ROM requires only SCSI support. All of the images support all mice, SLIP, CSLIP, PPP, FPU emulation, all filesystems except *extfs* and *xiafs*, console selection, ELF, SysV IPC, IP forwarding, firewalling and accounting, reverse ARP, and parallel printer support.

None of the images have QIC tape support or sound card support. After the installation is complete you may want to rebuild a kernel that only includes the support you need. See the section called "Rebuilding the Kernel" in Chapter 4, *Post-Installation Configuration* for more information on how to build your own kernel.

Making floppies under DOS

After choosing a kernel configuration, write the corresponding boot image *bootXXXX.img* file to the first floppy disk and label it. You can do this using the *rawrite* command under DOS. You would execute something like (assuming your CD is drive `d:`):

```
d:\dosutils\rawrite.exe
```

It will ask you for a filename to write. Enter the *bootXXXX.img* that you recorded earlier. It will then ask for a drive. This should always be `a:`.

To make the ramdisks, back up one directory level (*cd ..*) and run *rawrite* again. When prompted for a file name, enter *ramdisk1.img*. Again, enter `a:` for the drive name and continue. After this disk is done, repeat the above steps (with a new disk in the drive) and enter *ramdisk2.img* for the image to write. You should now have three disks labeled *boot*, *ramdisk1*, and *ramdisk2*.

Making floppies under Linux

If you already have Linux installed, making your boot disks is easy. Enter the following commands (assuming you have mounted your CD–ROM on */mnt/cdrom*):

```
cd /mnt/cdrom/images
./mkfloppies.pl
```

The *mkfloppies.pl* script asks you about your hardware and makes the proper disks based on the answers. If possible, it also saves some of your configuration information such as network addresses, X configuration, etc. You will then be prompted with those numbers as the default values during the installation.

Preparing for NFS, FTP, and Floppy Installs

- *NFS.* If you wish to install over a network, you will need to mount the RHC Linux CD–ROM on a machine that supports ISO–9660 filesystems with Rock Ridge extensions. The machine must also support NFS. Export the CD–ROM filesystem via NFS. Use the same boot and ramdisks to do a network installation. You will need to know the NFS server's IP address and the path to the exported CD–ROM.
- *FTP.* For an FTP installation, use the same boot disk and ramdisks. You will need to have a valid nameserver configured, or you will need the IP address of the FTP server you are using. You will also need the path to the root of the Red Hat directory.
- *Floppy.* For a floppy installation, you use the same boot disk and ramdisks, but you also need to make a bunch of other floppies. Use the same method to make the floppies as you used to make the boot/ramdisks. You need to get the image files either off a CD-ROM or via FTP and write them to their own floppies. There are a lot of floppies, so it is important to label them well. You need to get *main.img* and then get each of the images from the directories for each series you want to installation, for example, each of the images from the *Base* directory. If you want networking, get all of the images from the *Networking* directory. Write each of these images to its own disk using the same method you used to write your boot/ramdisks. To do the installation, just follow the instructions normally. The only noticeable difference (apart from

speed), is that from time to time (especially during package installation) the installation script will ask you to insert a particular floppy disk.

Booting the Installation System

Boot your machine off the boot floppy you just created. You will first see the `LILO boot:` prompt. The first time through, just press the Enter key. Watch the messages as the Linux kernel initializes your hardware. If the kernel boots and recognizes all your hardware properly you are set! If it misses something or gets something wrong, you may need to enter some parameters at the `LILO boot:` prompt, or use a different boot image. If you do need to specify some parameters, remember them—you will need them later.

Boot Disk Message

Here is the message that appears when you first boot the boot disk. We have added numbers in the left–hand column so we can talk about each line.

```
 1                        Red Hat Linux 2.1
 2
 3 You are at the LILO boot prompt. If Linux is having trouble properly
 4 detecting your hardware, try setting some hardware parameters here.
 5
 6 IDE Hard Drives                      hd[a,b,c,d]=cylinders,heads,sectors
 7 Mitsumi CD-ROM                       mcd=port,irq
 8 Sony 31&33 CD-ROM REQUIRED           cdu31a=base_addr,[irq|0][,PAS]
 9 Aztech CD268                         aztcd=port
10 Ethernet Card                        ether=irq,base_addr,mem_start,mem_end
11 Bus Mouse                            bmouse=irq
12 SCSI Seagate ST0x                    st0x=base_addr,irq
13 SCSI Future Domain TMC-8xx           tmc8xx=base_addr,irq
14 SCSI Trantor T128                    t128=base_addr,irq
15 SCSI NCR-5380 Based                  ncr5380=port,irq,dma_channel
16 Adaptec 15{1,2}x, SoundBlasterSCSI   aha152x=port,irq,scsi_id,reconnect,pa
17 Adaptec 1542                         aha1542=base_addr
18 Buslogic                             buslogic=base_addr
19 Pro Audio Spectrum / Studio 16       pas16=port,irq
20 SoundBlaster Pro or 16 compatible    sbpcd=io_addr,{SoundBlaster,Lasermate
21 ATAPI/IDE CD-ROM Drives              hd{a,b,c,d}=cdrom
22          (all addresses (not IRQs) should begin with 0x; i.e., 0x340)
23 Enter "linux <param> <param> ..." (or just hit ENTER to auto-detect).
```

Here is a close examination of each line in the message:

Line 1: Our name and the version you have.

Lines 3–4: Brief instructions.

Line 6: This line is almost never necessary and should be used only as a last resort. If your hard drives are not being recognized or are giving odd errors, you can try these parameters. If your first hard drive is acting up, enter:

```
linux hda=xxx,xxx,xxx
```

where the xxx represents your parameters from BIOS. When a parameter has commas, make sure you do not put a space after the commas. The only spaces on the command line should be after *linux* and between multiple parameters (e.g., *linux mcd=0x340,11 bmouse=5*).

Line 7: Use this if your Mitsumi CD–ROM is not recognized properly. For example, *linux mcd=0x340,11*.

Line 8: This line is required for the sony cdu31a or 33a. Use `cdu31a` for *both* the 31 and the 33 (i.e., do *not* use `cdu33a` as a parameter on the command line). For example, *linux cdu31a=0x340,0*.

Line 9: If you have an Aztech CD268, try *linux aztcd=0x340* (or whatever your port is).

Line 10: If your ethernet card is not recognized, you can try to use these parameters. For an ethernet card on base address 0x340 and irq 10, enter *linux ether=10,0x340*.

Line 11: If your bus mouse isn't recognized, try this parameter.

Line 12: For an old Seagate ST0x controller, use this parameter.

Line 13: For a Future Domain TMC–8xx controller, use this parameter.

Line 14: For a trantor T128, use this line.

Line 15: For an NCR–5380, use this line. For a card at 0x330 and IRQ 11 and DMA 5, you would use *linux ncr5380=0x330,11,5*.

Line 16: Use this line for an Adaptec 1505, 1510, 1515, 1520, and 1522 (and Sound Blaster SCSI). The reconnect and parity are optional. For a CD–ROM hooked to ID 1 and a controller with a base address of 0x330 and IRQ 11 you would use:

```
linux aha152x=0x330,11,1,reconnect,parity
```

Line 17: Use this if you are having problems with an Adaptec 1542 (rare).

Line 18: Use this if you are having trouble with a Buslogic controller (also rare).

Line 19: Use this for Pro Audio Spectrums and Pro Audio Studio cards that aren't recognized.

Line 20: Use this if you have the "normal" Sound Blaster CD interface and it doesn't work. This is the regular run–of–the–mill Sound Blaster type that controls the Panasonic 56x drives, Matsushta Kotobuki drives, TEAC CD55A, and a few others. If you have a Sound Blaster with something like the Panasonic connected using base address 0x240, you would use *linux sbpcd=0x240,SoundBlaster.*

Line 21: If you have an IDE (ATAPI compliant) CD–ROM that is not recognized by the autoprobe, you can use this parameter to tell it where to look. Normally, if you have IDE hard drives, they take up the first available drive letters. If you had 2 IDE hard drives, your CD–ROM would be hdc. If you had one IDE hard drive, it would be hdb. It's usually okay to just try them all. You would use *linux hdb=CD–ROM* if you had one IDE hard drive.

Line 22: A reminder that you must put a `0x` in front of all Hex values (such as base addresses).

Line 23: Instructions on what to enter.

When you see the "VFS: Insert ramdisk floppy . . . " message, insert the ramdisk1 floppy and press Enter. After a minute or so, you will be prompted for the ramdisk2 disk. Insert it and press the Enter key. If all goes well you will be presented with the welcome dialog box.

Using the Dialog Boxes

Use of the dialog boxes is quite simple. In most dialog boxes there is a "cursor" or "highlight bar" which you can move around with your arrow keys and the Tab key. If you are presented with a menu of items from which you are supposed to select one, move the highlight bar over the item you wish to select, and press Enter. If you are presented with a list of items and you are supposed to select any number of items (a *checklist*) move the highlight bar and press the space bar to select an item. To deselect an item, press the space bar again. Press Enter when you are done selecting items.

Boot Floppy

When the installation script loads, it asks you to insert the boot disk. Remove the second ramdisk and insert the original boot disk, then press Enter.

Installation Type

You will now be offered a choice of five installation methods.

- *CD–ROM.* If you have a CD–ROM drive with the Red Hat CD.
- *NFS.* If you have an NS server with the Red Hat CD (or a mirror).
- *Local Hard Drive.* If you copied the Red Hat files to one of your hard drives.

- *FTP.* If you want to install directly from an FTP server.
- *Floppy Disks.* If you are installing via floppy disks.

If you select CD–ROM or NFS installations, you will be asked if you want to do an X–based (graphical) or text–based installation. You should at least try to do the X–based installation. It is much easier to tailor your system to your needs this way, because package selection can be done at a package-by-package level. With a text installation you can only select certain "series" of packages. The X installation is also a little more intuitive.

If the X installation fails, you can always drop back and do the text installation. The other three installation methods require a text–based installation.

Disk Partitions

The purpose of partitions is explained in *Running Linux.* You need at least one partition for all the Linux files and another for swap space. Serious Linux users will probably want more partitions, so they can do things like separate the space used by system utilities from user files.

You can create partitions with the *fdisk* that comes with any operating system. But you must still run the Linux version of *fdisk* at installation time to tag your swap partition as "Linux swap" and your other partitions as "Linux native." This is because other *fdisk* programs know how to tag partition types just for their own operating system.

There is a fundamental part of this partitioning process that you *must* get right. You must tag your partitions properly. When you use *fdisk* to create your partitions, each new partition will have a default type of `Linux Native`. This is fine for all Linux partitions, but you will need to change it for your swap partition. You need it to be partition type 82, or `Linux Swap`. Even if you create your partitions with some other software (i.e., the OS/2 *fdisk*), you must still use the Linux *fdisk* to tag the partitions to the proper type.

The next screen lets you choose between *fdisk* or *cfdisk*. *cfdisk* has been known to be buggy in certain situations, but it usually works fine. It is recommended that you use *cfdisk*, and only resort to *fdisk* if *cfdisk* gives you problems. Select the one you want to use with the arrow keys and press Enter.

A list of drives found on your system is then displayed. Select a drive to partition. After partitioning that drive you will be offered the chance to partition another drive.

We recommend a configuration such as this:

1. If you have 8M of RAM, make a 16–24M swap partition (depending on how much you plan to do with Linux at one time). If you have 16M or more of RAM, just make as much swap as you have RAM.

2. Make a 30M / partition
3. Make a 150M (or more depending on how much you want to install) */usr* partition. If you plan to install everything, this should be more like 350M.
4. If you plan to install a lot of the source (which is not required), you may want to make a */usr/src* partition as well of about 200M.
5. Make a 50M or so */home* partition. This is where all user's home directories go, so you are completely at your own discretion on size for this one (although 50M is a good number for a single user system, 200M may be too much for a 4 user system).
6. You may want a 50M or so */usr/local* partition as well for software that doesn't come from RPMs.

While creating partitions, it is a good idea to write down which partitions are meant for which filesystems.

Creating different partitions allows you to more easily back up your data and will also allow you to move your data around more easily should you need to increase partition sizes. If you are using a lot of source, it's much easier to move 200M of stuff somewhere else, repartition, and move it back than it is to move a 600M root partition somewhere!

After exiting the partitioning program, if you see a message like "Re–read table failed with error . . . " you will need to reboot your machine so that Linux can reload the partition table data. This generally happens if you create, change, or delete any extended partitions. If you need to reboot, do so, and go through all the same steps you did to get to the partitioning step, but then skip the partitioning step (you've already done it).

Once you are done partitioning, the installation will probe for swap partitions. If it does find one, it will ask you if you want to initialize it. It is a very good idea to do so now.

Configure Networking

Choose `Yes` if you have an ethernet card and wish to have that card activated at boot time. Choose `No` if you have a standalone machine or network only over a serial line via PPP or SLIP.

If you choose `No`, you can skip this section and go on to the next one.

If you choose `Yes`, you will be presented with several menus to install networking. You will need to know several network parameters for your machine. Sometimes defaults will be provided. Table 3-1 lists the parameters that are requested and some example values. *These are only examples—do not use these parameters!*

Table 3-1: Networking Parameters

Parameter	Example
Hostname	elroy
Domain Name	redhat.com
FQDN	elroy.redhat.com
IP Address	199.183.24.5
Network Address	199.183.24.0
Network Mask	255.255.255.0
Broadcast Address	199.183.24.255
Default Gateway	199.192.24.1
Nameserver	199.183.24.101

After entering the parameters, you will have the opportunity to review them and change them before committing to them.

Setup Media

- *CD–ROM Installation.* At this point, the CD–ROM devices are probed in an attempt to find the Red Hat media. If all goes well, one will be found and the CD will be mounted. If it fails, that means one of several things could have gone wrong:

  1. You picked the wrong boot image and the one you are using doesn't have support for your particular CD–ROM. In this case, you'll need to go back to DOS and remake your boot disk using a more appropriate image.
  2. You picked the right boot image, but for some reason the kernel didn't detect your hardware. In this case, you'll need to reboot and try and specify hardware parameters.
  3. You have a SCSI CD–ROM and your controller card was not recognized properly. This could be due to having the wrong boot image or due to the need for hardware parameters at the LILO prompt.
  4. You forgot to insert the CD–ROM in the drive.

- *NFS Installation.* If you haven't configured networking already, you must do so now. After that, you will be prompted for a server and a mount point. It's a good idea to use IP addresses for the server, but if you have configured a good nameserver with your networking, a hostname should work. You will then need to enter the mount path. If all goes well, your media will be mounted and you can go on to the section called "Continuing a Text Installation". If the mount fails, you either configured networking wrong, or your server is refusing to allow you to mount. Try to make sure networking is correct, and then make sure you can mount the server from another machine.

- *FTP Installation.* If you pick the FTP installation, you will be presented with a list of known FTP sites. Try one of these sites or use your own by selecting `Other` and entering your own site. In this case, you will have to know the path to the Red Hat directory. At this point, you can continue with the section called "Continuing a Text Installation".
- *Floppy Installation.* You will be prompted to insert the "main" disk out of the floppy series. This disk is used to find out series information, etc. Once you are done, you can go on to the section called "Continuing a Text Installation".
- *Local Hard Drive Installation.* You will now be asked to enter the device where your Red Hat files are stored on your hard drive. You also must enter the filesystem type (i.e., `msdos` for DOS filesystems, etc.). Once you enter this and your files are found, you can continue to the section called "Continuing a Text Installation".

Continuing the Installation

If you are doing an X installation, continue by reading the section called "Graphical Installation".

If you are doing a text, FTP, local hard drive, or floppy installation, go on to the section called "Continuing a Text Installation".

Graphical Installation

To do the graphical install, you first have to configure X for your system. You can follow the instructions for X Configuration in the section called "X Window System Configuration" in Chapter 4. Please note that if *Xconfigurator* doesn't properly configure X, you can *not* use *xf86config*. You will have to go back and do the text–based installation instead, and then configure X with *xf86config* when you get your machine installed and rebooted.

You may have to wait a minute or two for X to start, depending on your network or your CD–ROM speed. If X starts properly, you will get a screen with a window in the upper left asking you to press a button if everything looks OK. If it does, click on the button. Otherwise, you can wait for it to time out (it takes 30 seconds), or you can press Control–Alt–backspace to kill X. At that point, you can try to configure X again, or you can do the text installation.

Choosing Partitions

If you have only one partition of the type "Linux native," you will see a window telling you that since you have only one mountable partition it will use that for your root filesystem.

If you have more than one partition of the type "Linux native," you will be presented with a menu of options as shown in Figure 3-1, from which you need to select a "root partition." The root partition is where you store the root (/) filesystem. Select the root partition by clicking on it. Then click the `Done` button.

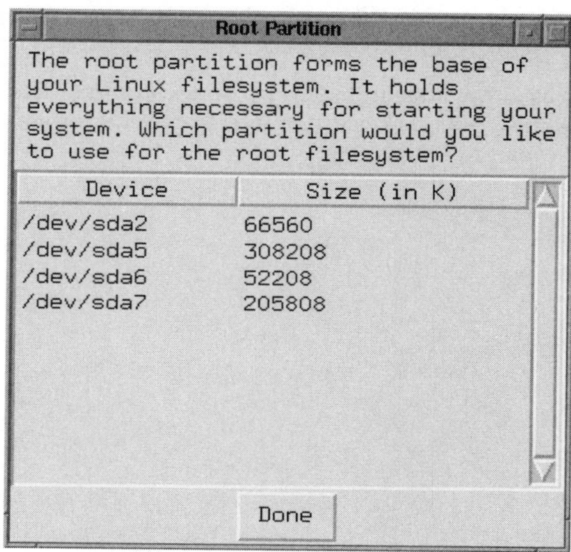

Figure 3-1. Root filesystem selection

Selecting Partitions

You will be presented with a list of partitions on your system. For each partition you want to mount, select it with your mouse and click `Edit`. This will bring up another window, like the one in Figure 3-2, that will let you define a mount point for the partition (e.g., */usr*). Type in the mount point, including the leading `/`.

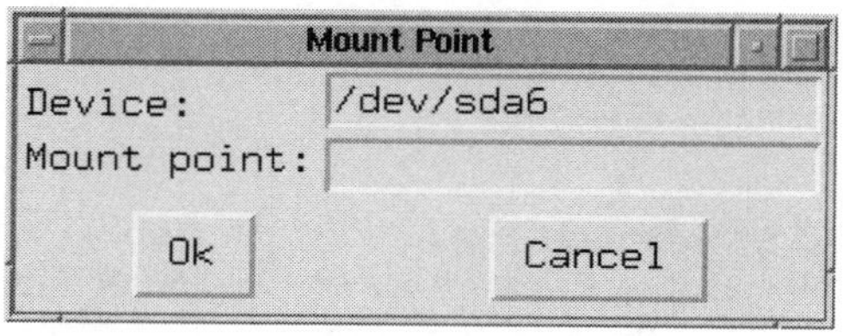

Mount Point

Device: /dev/sda6

Mount point:

Ok Cancel

Figure 3-2. Edit mount point

Formatting Partitions

The next step asks you which partitions you would like to format. The window will be similar to that shown in Figure 3-3. You *must* format all partitions on to which you plan to install RHCL. However, none are selected by default. This is to ensure that you don't accidentally format partitions that you may not have meant to.

If you have partitions from a previous Linux system that you wish to preserve (like a */home* partition), do not select them. If you do select them, they will be formatted and you will lose your data.

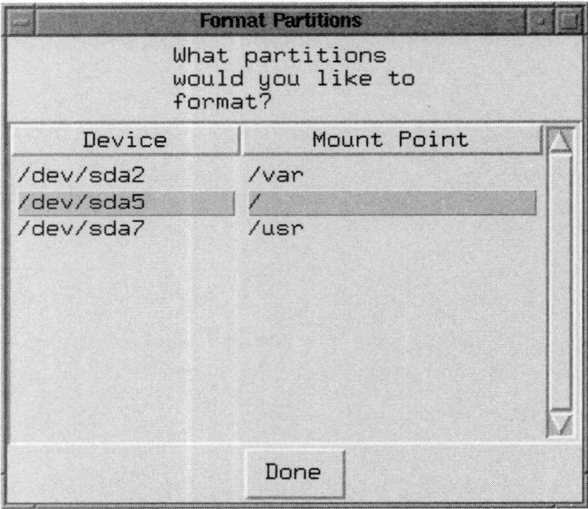

Figure 3–3. Format partitions

Click the mouse button on each partition you want to format. Then click the `Done` button. You will see a series of small windows indicating that your partitions are being formatted.

Select Packages

You are now at the point where you select your software packages. A window is displayed (Figure 3-4) that will let you select some software in groups. Selecting everything here *does not* select everything in the RHCL system. Once you pick the groups you want, you will be presented with a window that looks like a file manager (Figure 3-5). You will see some folders with numbers and the occasional `All` printed on the folder. This tells you how many packages are selected in the folder. The bottom of the window tells you the disk space requirements for all the selected packages.

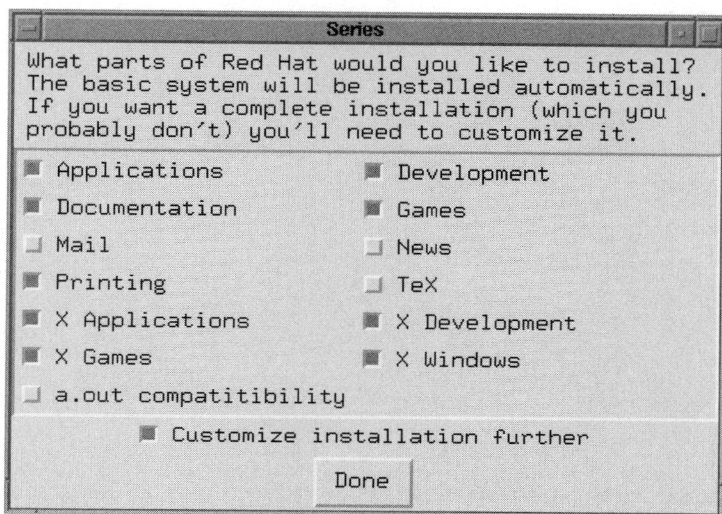

Figure 3-4. Series selection

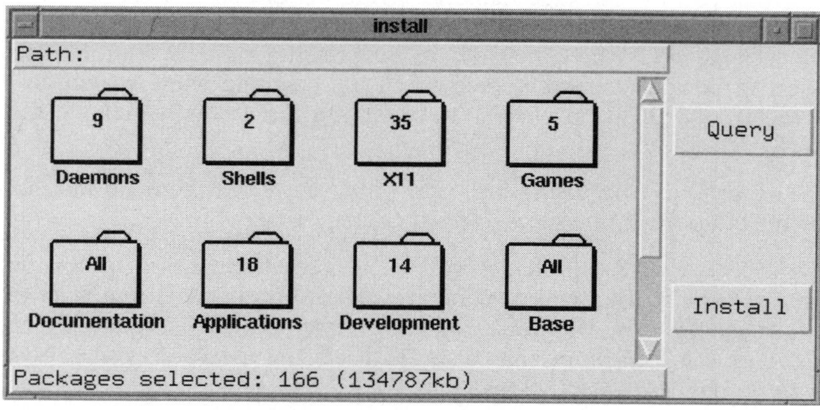

Figure 3-5. Main customization window

You can move around in the package selection window much like a file manager. Double-click on folders to open them, and double-click on the `Back` folder to go back up a level. To select more or to unselect some packages, simply click on the folder you want to change. Then find the package you want to select or deselect and click on it. Make sure you have more available disk space than you have selected packages. You can see the disk space requirement at the bottom of the window change as you select and deselect packages. See Figure 3-6 for an example of actual selected packages.

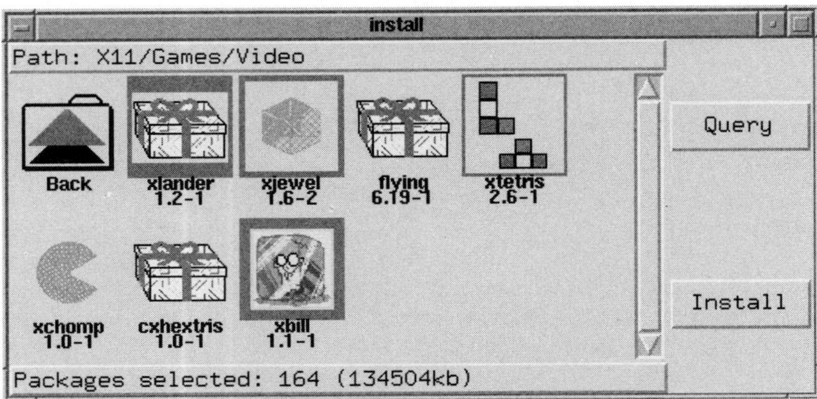

Figure 3-6. Choosing packages

Your right mouse button creates a pop–up menu when pressed over a folder or a package. This menu allows you to select and unselect folders or packages, but it also allows you to "query" individual packages. If you query a package, you are given a window that lists the package name, description, and the file list. You can also select or unselect the package from here, as well as get more details, such as who built the package and when they did it, by pressing `Details` button. This works for folders of packages as well, except that the resulting window will give you a list on the left of all the packages and you can flip through them in the query window.

You can do the same "querying" using the button on the right of the main installation window. This button will query *all* selected packages.

Once you have selected all the packages you want, click the `Install` button on the main window. A dialog box with two bar graphs displays the current state of the package installation. The top bar represents the current package being installed, and the bottom bar represents all packages being installed. Also shown are the package numbers, total kilobytes installed, and an estimated time for the installation.

Finishing Up

After you've selected the packages and they are all installed, there are just a few more steps to do. You first need to indicate which time system you want to use. UTC is the international standard, and if you use it your machine will handle daylight savings time properly, and moving from time zone to time zone will be a breeze. If you will be connected to a network, you should use UTC. Otherwise, Local Time is fine.

After that, you will need to select your time zone. Just click on the zone you are in. Then select your keyboard mapping from the available list. Users in the United States, for instance, will choose `us.map`.

Then you'll need to install LILO, the LInux LOader. LILO is a small program that lets you choose between different operating systems when your computer boots. A window asks you where you want to install it. For most people, this is on the MBR of their first physical hard drive. You can also specify other operating systems for LILO to use. Once you've answered all the questions, you should be presented with a *lilo.conf* for reviewing. Hopefully, the worst thing that will happen is that Linux will be the only operating system you can boot. If this happens, you can read the LILO–FAQ in */usr/doc/FAQ* to find out how to fix LILO to boot other operating systems (such as DOS).

That's it . . . you're now ready to reboot. Skip the following sections and go to the section called "Rebooting Your Machine".

Continuing a Text Installation

If you are installing without the use of the X Window System interface, you should follow the directions in this section.

Select Filesystems for Format

You will now be presented with a list of partitions to format. Use the arrow keys and the space bar to select all the partitions you need to format. Do not select partitions that contain data you want to keep.

Mount Filesystems

You now need to select which filesystems to mount and where. You should be presented with a list of all partitions that were tagged as "Linux Native." You need to select `Add`, and then select one of the partitions to use for a root partition. Continue adding partitions if necessary (if you are mounting in a separate */usr* directory, etc.).

You may not be prompted with this step at all if you only have one partition of type "Linux Native," since that must be the one to use.

Package Installation

At this point, you must select the groups of software you want to install. You do so by moving the highlight bar with the arrow keys to the item you want to select and pressing the Space bar on that item. When you have checked everything that you want, press Enter.

You will then see a `Package Installation` window that shows a bar graph of all the packages as they install.

Kernel Installation

After the packages have been installed, the installation program will copy the kernel from the boot floppy to your new Linux system. This will take about theru a minute on most systems, so be patient.

Mouse Configuration

Just pick the mouse on the list that matches your hardware. If you have a serial mouse, you will next select which serial (COM) port to use.

Network Configuration

If you are doing an NFS or FTP installation, networking should already be configured at this point. You will be asked if you want to use those parameters for your installed system. If for some reason you do not want to use those parameters (for instance, if your machine is normally connected to another network, or not connected at all), you will have the opportunity to reconfigure networking.

If you are doing a CD–ROM, floppy, or hard drive installation, and you want networking, you will need to configure networking now. See the section called "Configure Networking", earlier in this chapter, for information on how to configure networking properly, then return here.

Otherwise, just answer `No` when asked if you want to install networking and continue.

Modem Configuration

If you have a modem, you must tell the system which serial (COM) port it is on. This step simply makes a link from */dev/modem* to the proper device under Linux so that programs like *minicom* will work with little configuration.

Clock Configuration

Next you will be asked if you want to use Local Time or GMT/UTC style time. UTC is the international standard, and if you use it your machine will handle daylight savings time properly, and moving from time zone to time zone will be a breeze. If you will be connected to a network, you should use UTC. Otherwise, Local Time is fine.

Next, you will be asked for a time zone. Scroll through the list (using the arrow keys) until you find your time zone and then press Enter.

Select Keymap

For most systems, just press Enter. If you do not use a U.S.-style keyboard, move the highlight bar (using the arrow keys) to the type you are using and press Enter.

LILO Installation

You should install LILO to boot your Linux system, unless you do not want to overwrite your MBR, and you have another way to boot your Linux system. Installing LILO is quite safe and is recommended.

If you choose to install it, you are asked where you want to install LILO on your hard drive. On most systems, you will want to install to the MBR of the first physical disk. Some people using "Boot Manager" from OS/2 or something similar might want to install LILO to the superblock of the root partition.

Next you will be asked if you need to specify hardware parameters. If you had to type something at the `LILO boot:` prompt to get your system to install properly, you will probably want to put that here. Otherwise, select `No`. If you select `Yes`, type the parameters in the next window and press Enter.

Next you will be asked if you want to boot another operating system from LILO. If you do, answer `Yes`. If not, answer `No`. If you answered `Yes`, you must now specify what type of partition to use. Continue by telling it exactly what you want to boot.

Creating User Accounts

If you want to start with some user accounts, create them now. It is recommended that you create a user account for yourself. To add a user, you first enter an account name. This must be a single "word" with no spaces, and ideally should be limited to 8 characters. As an example, "djb" is a good account name. You have the option of *not* creating a home directory for the user. If you have an existing */home* partition, or if you will be mounting */home* over NFS, you may not want a */home* directory to be created.

The user accounts that you create here will have their passwords "locked," preventing those users from logging in. To enable those accounts you must log in as root, and run `passwd` *`account`* to set a password for each account.

Root Password

Enter your root password here. At all costs, make it something you will remember. Your password will need to mix numerals and upper- and lowercase characters.

You are now done with installation, but we recommend that you reboot.

Rebooting Your Machine

Once the installation is completed, you will be presented with the option to reboot the machine. Remove the disks from the floppy drive (otherwise, the system will boot from the floppy disk), and reboot. Provided everything went well and you installed LILO, you should get a `LILO boot:` prompt. Here you can do several things:

- Press Enter to boot the default OS (Linux).
- Press Tab to see a list of possible OSs to boot.
- Type the name of an alternate OS (like "dos").

The operating system you select will be booted.

CHAPTER FOUR

Post-Installation Configuration

After installation your system is fully functional, but you may still want to do some additional configuration. This chapter describes some of the various system configuration tasks you may need to do.

Package Installation (or Uninstallation)

Remember that even if you selected every series available, there are still software packages on the CD–ROM that are not installed on your system. You can use RPM or glint to install additional packages. See Chapter 6, *Package Management with RPM*, and Chapter 9, *Glint*, for introductions to RPM and glint, respectively.

X Window System Configuration

There are three methods for configuring the X Window System on your machine: *Xconfigurator*, *xf86config*, or by hand. None of them are foolproof, and each will do a better job than the others for some combinations of hardware. Unfortunately, that is the state of X configuration for Linux—you just have to try it and see if it works. If you are unsure of anything in this process, a good source of extra documentation is *http://www.xfree86.org*.

Xconfigurator is a full–screen menu-driven program that walks you through the setup. *xf86config* is a line-oriented program distributed with XFree86. It isn't as easy to use as *Xconfigurator*, but it usually works in cases where the latter fails. If both fail, you may have an unsupported card or you may need to write the config file by hand. Usually the former is the case, so check and make sure your card is supported before attempting to write the config file yourself.

All of this is moot, however, if you did the X–based install. The X–based install copies the config file that it used to your installed system. You should be able to reboot from the X install, log in, and run *startx*.

The X Server

Provided you selected the proper chipset type at install time, you should have the proper X server installed and linked in. When later running *Xconfigurator* or *xf86config*, you need to make sure you select this same chipset or the autoprobe will fail.

If you think you installed the wrong X server for your chipset, you will have to install the right one before you can configure it. To do so, execute the following commands (assuming the Red Hat CD–ROM is mounted on */mnt/cdrom*, and that you need to install the S3 server):

```
cd /mnt/cdrom/RedHat/RPMS
rpm -ivh XFree86-S3-3.1.2-1.i386.rpm
ln -sf /usr/X11R6/bin/XF86_S3 /usr/X11R6/bin/X
```

This will install the S3 server and make the proper link.

Xconfigurator

Xconfigurator is simple to use, although it does require a little knowledge on your part. You will need to know what type of chipset your card has. For example, most newer Diamond cards use the S3 chipset, so you would want to install the S3 server for those. An ET–4000, however, would use the generic SVGA server.

Selecting your server

If you are unsure what chipset you have, the best way to find out is usually to look at the card itself. This is unnecessary in most cases, but sometimes it is the only way. Table 4-1 lists which chipsets and boards require which servers. Pick the one that best matches your hardware.

Table 4–1: X Servers

Server	Chipset
VGA16	All VGA boards with 256K (16-color only)
SVGA	Trident 8900 & 9400, Cirrus Logic, C & T, ET4000, others
Mach8	ATI boards using the Mach8 chipset
Mach32	ATI boards using the Mach32 chipset
Mach64	ATI boards using the Mach64 chipset
8514	IBM 8514/A boards and true clones
S3	#9 Boards, most Diamonds, some Orchids, others

Table 4-1: X Servers (continued)

Server	Chipset
AGX	All XGA graphics boards
P9000	Diamond Viper (but not the 9100) and others
W32	All ET4000/W32 cards, but not standard ET4000s

Selecting your mouse

This is fairly self explanatory. Just pick the one that matches your hardware.

Finishing up

The Xconfigurator does something called an autoprobe, which tries to figure out what your hardware is and choose the right configuration options. From here, you should be able to just autoprobe and have everything else you need detected. If this fails, you'll need to run *xf86config*. You'll know this failed if you are asked questions that you don't know the answer to. These questions are usually things like "Please enter your clocks" or "Which ramdac do you have?".

Assuming everything goes fine for your card, you will be asked to select a monitor. There are many monitors in our database, but not *every* monitor. If your monitor isn't listed, you should pick "Generic Monitor" or "Generic Multisync." The former is for straight VGA resolution monitors, the latter for monitors that do up to 1024x768. You may find Generic Multisync lacking because it only does 1024x768 in interlaced mode. This is for protection to make sure you don't accidentally select something that could damage your monitor.

If later you want to increase the refresh rate for your monitor, you can edit the config file by hand or you can run *Xconfigurator* again and pick a monitor from our list that more closely matches the specs of your monitor.

Once the monitor is selected, you will be asked which video modes you would like to use. Here you can select multiple modes using your arrow keys and space bar. Sometimes people want multiple modes for viewing pictures, etc. This enables you to actually configure X for multiple modes and then switch video modes while X is running using `ControlAlt+` and `ControlAlt-`.

The next screen will ask you which of the selected modes you want to be your primary mode. Simply highlight the one you want to be your default mode and press Enter. When you start X that will be your mode. To switch, use `ControlAlt` and `+` or `-`.

xf86config

xf86config is fairly self–documenting, with plenty of text describing its operation throughout the program. It should yield a working */etc/XF86Config* file (which you should move to */etc/X11/XF86Config*). It is worth noting that *xf86config* will ask you if you want it to set a link for you. This should be unnecessary on a Red Hat system.

Sendmail

A default *sendmail.cf* file will be installed in */etc*. The default configuration should work for most SMTP–only sites. It will *not* work for UUCP sites; you will need to generate a new *sendmail.cf* if you need to use UUCP mail transfers.

To generate a new *sendmail.cf*, you will need to install *m4* and the sendmail source package. Read the *README* in the sendmail sources for more details on creating *sendmail* configuration files. Also, O'Reilly & Associates publishes a good sendmail reference called *sendmail*, by Bryan Costales.

One common sendmail configuration is to have a single machine act as a mail gateway for all the machines on your network. For instance, at Red Hat Software we have a machine called **mail.redhat.com** that does all our mail. On that machine we simply need to add the names of machines for which **mail.redhat.com** will handle mail to */etc/sendmail.cw*. Here is an example:

```
# sendmail.cw - include all aliases for your machine here.
torgo.redhat.com
poodle.redhat.com
devel.redhat.com
```

Then on the other machines, **torgo**, **poodle**, and **devel**, we need to edit */etc/sendmail.cf* to "masquerade" as **mail.redhat.com** when sending mail, and to forward any local mail processing to **redhat.com**. Find the `DH` and `DM` lines in */etc/sendmail.cf* and edit them thusly:

```
# who gets all local email traffic
DHredhat.com
# who I masquerade as (null for no masquerading)
DMredhat.com
```

With this type of configuration, all mail sent will appear as if it were sent from **mail.redhat.com** and any mail sent to **torgo.redhat.com** or the other hosts, will be delivered to **mail.redhat.com**.

Controlling Access to Services

As a security measure, most network services are managed by a protective program called a *TCP wrapper*. The protected services are those listed in */etc/inetd.conf* that specify */usr/sbin/tcpd*. *tcpd* can allow or deny access to a service based on the origin of the request, and the configuration in */etc/hosts.allow* and */etc/hosts.deny*.

By default Red Hat Linux allows all service requests. To disable or limit services you can edit */etc/hosts.allow*. Here is an example */etc/hosts.allow* file:

```
ALL: redhat.com .redhat.com
in.talkd: ALL
in.ntalkd: ALL
in.fingerd: ALL
in.ftpd: ALL
```

This configuration allows all connections from **redhat.com** and ***.redhat.com** machines. It also allows *talk*, *finger*, and *ftp* requests from all machines.

tcpd allows much more sophisticated access control, using a combination of */etc/hosts.allow* and */etc/hosts.deny*. Read the *tcpd*(8) and *hosts_access*(5) man pages for complete details.

Anonymous FTP

Setting up anonymous FTP is simple. All you need to do is install the *anon–ftp* RPM package (which you may have already done at install time). Once it is installed, anonymous FTP will be up and running.

There are a few files you might wish to edit to configure your FTP server.

/etc/ftpaccess
: This file defines most of the access control for your FTP server. Some of the things that you can do are set up logical "groups" to control access from different sites, limit the number of simultaneous FTP connections, and configure transfer logging. Read the *ftpaccess* man page for complete details.

/etc/ftphosts
: The *ftphosts* file is used to allow or deny access to certain accounts from various hosts. Read the *ftphosts* man page for details.

/etc/ftpusers
: This file lists all the users that are *not* allowed to ftp into your machine. For example, `root` is listed in */etc/ftpusers* by default. That means that you can not ftp to your machine, and log in as root. This is a good security measure, but some administrators prefer to remove `root` from this file.

World Wide Web Server

If you installed the Apache web server (from the *apache* package), then your web service is already up and running! Just point your web browser at *http://localhost.*

The default page that is shown is */home/httpd/html/index.html.* You can edit this file (or completely replace it) to your liking. All the CGI programs, icons, and HTML pages are stored in */home/httpd,* but this can be changed in the Apache configuration files, all of which are stored in */etc/httpd/conf.* Logs of all httpd activity are kept in */var/log/httpd.*

Configuration of your web server is beyond the scope of this manual. There are a number of good books available that can help you configure your web server for your site.

NFS Configuration

All the required NFS deamons are started at boot time by default, but the *portmapper,* which controls access to NFS services, utilizes the */etc/hosts.allow* and */etc/hosts.deny* files for access control. The default installation enables all portmap service requests, but you may wish to disable or restrict such services. To do so, edit */etc/hosts.allow* and use `portmap: pattern` lines to control connections to *portmap.*

In order to avoid deadlocks, the *portmap* program does not attempt to look up the remote hostname or username, nor will it try to match NIS net groups. The upshot of all this is that only network number patterns will work for portmap access control. For example, to allow all hosts in the **redhat.com** domain (whose network address is 199.183.24.0), you would add the following line to */etc/hosts.allow*:

```
portmap: 199.183.24.0/255.255.255.0
```

See the *hosts_access*(5) and *rpc.portmap*(8) man pages for complete access control details.

To actually export a filesystem edit */etc/exports.* For example,

```
/mnt/rhscd          *.redhat.com(ro)
/mnt/cdrom          *.redhat.com(ro)
```

allows hosts matching ***.redhat.com** to mount */mnt/rhscd* and */mnt/cdrom* read–only. After editing */etc/exports* you will have to kill and restart the *rpc.nfsd* and *rpc.mountd* daemons so they will load the new configuration. This can be done by issuing:

```
/etc/rc.d/init.d/nfs stop
/etc/rc.d/init.d/nfs start
```

See the *exports*(5), *rpc.nfsd*(8) and *rpc.mountd*(8) man pages for complete NFS configuration details.

Rebuilding the Kernel

The best source of documentation on rebuilding your kernel should already be installed on your system. If you installed the *howto* package, you should be able to *cd* to */usr/doc/HOWTO* where you'll find tons of howto documents including the Kernel–HOWTO. They may be gzipped, so you may need to do something like *zcat Kernel–HOWTO | more.*

Running Programs at Boot Time

The file */etc/rc.d/rc.local* is executed at boot time, after all other initialization is complete. You can add additional initialization commands here. For instance, you may want to start up additional daemons, or initialize a printer. In addition, if you require serial port setup, you can add */etc/rc.d/rc.serial* and it will be executed automatically at boot time.

The default */etc/rc.d/rc.local* simply creates a nice login banner with your kernel version and machine type.

CHAPTER FIVE

FINDING DOCUMENTATION

Red Hat includes thousands of pages of online documentation to help you learn how to use the system. The man pages, information documents, and plain text files it includes provide information on almost every aspect of Linux. For more help, Red Hat also includes all of the documentation produced by the Linux Documentation Project electronically.

Man Pages

The most common form of documentation is man pages. There is a man page provided for most commands as well as many programming interfaces and configuration file formats. To read a man page, use the *man* command with the name of the man page to display as the argument. For example, to read about the *ls* command, use *man ls*. If you want to look up the arguments to the *read()* system call use *man read.*

Man Sections

The man pages are divided into nine sections:

Section	Contents
1	user commands
2	system calls
3	library calls
4	devices
5	file formats
6	games
7	miscellaneous

Section	Contents
8	system commands
9	kernel internals

By convention, the name of a man page is written as the man page title followed by its section number in parentheses. For example, the RPM man page is *rpm*(8).

Some items have man pages in multiple sections. To view the man page on an item from a particular section, give the section number as the first argument to man. So, to see the man page on *read* that's in section 3 (which covers the *read* command used by *tcl*), use this command:

```
man 3 read
```

Searching Man Pages

Red Hat's man page system includes a searching facility. To use it, you must have a *whatis* database set up. Red Hat systems rebuild this database nightly to keep it up-to-date. If you don't leave your machine on all night, though, it is likely that you don't have this database. To build one, use this command while logged in as root:

```
/usr/sbin/makewhatis /usr/man /usr/X11R6/man
```

You can now search your man pages through the *apropos* command (this is the same as *man –k*). Give the keyword you want to search on as its sole argument, and *apropos* returns a list of the man pages relating to that keyword along with a short description of that item.

A closely related command is *whatis*. It is run in the same manner as *man*, but it returns only a short description of the item asked about.

Info Documents

While *man* is the most ubiquitous documentation format, *info* is much more powerful. It provides hypertext links to make reading large documents much easier and many features for the documentation writer. There are some very complete *info* documents on various aspects of Red Hat (especially the portions from the GNU project).

To read *info* documentation, use the *info* command without any arguments. It will present you with a list of available documentation. If it can't find something, it's probably because you don't have the package installed that includes that documentation. Install it with RPM and try again.

If you're comfortable using emacs, it has a built-in browser for *info* documentation. Use `C-h C-i` to see the documentation (that's Control–h followed by Control–i).

The *info* system is a hypertext-based system. Any highlighted text that appears is a link leading to more information. Use the Tab key to move the cursor to the link, and press Enter to follow the link. Pressing `p` returns you to the previous page, `n` moves you to the next page, and `u` goes up one level of documentation. To exit *info*, press `C-x C-c`.

The best way to learn how to use *info* is to read the info documentation on it. If you read the first screen that *info* presents you'll be able to get started.

Linux Documentation Project

The Linux Documentation Project (LDP) is a group of Linux users working on high quality documentation. For more information on it, point a web browser at *http://sunsite.unc.edu/linux.html.*

Text

The text versions of the Linux Documentation Project documents are in */usr/doc/FAQ* and */usr/doc/HOWTO*. They are compressed to save space, but can be easily read with *zmore*.

World Wide Web

The LDP documents are also provided in a form that can easily be read with a web browser. Use the URL *file://localhost/usr/doc/HTML/index.html* to do so.

Other Documentation

Red Hat places any documentation on a package that's not in *man* or *info* formats in */usr/doc*. Each package has its own subdirectory containing all of the documentation.

CHAPTER SIX

Package Management with RPM

Red Hat Linux is a complex system composed of many software packages. These packages are always being improved with new features and bug fixes. In order to keep your system up-to-date, you'll want to get new versions of this software, but you don't want to reinstall your entire system to upgrade. A package manager can cleanly upgrade individual software packages without disturbing the rest of the system.

RPM stand for Red Hat Package Manager. With RPM, you can install and uninstall software packages. You can also track your installed packages, verify that they are installed correctly, and query them for information (like install date, size, etc.).

While RPM does contain "Red Hat" in the name, we want it to be an open packaging system, so it is redistributable under the terms of the GPL. Red Hat Software encourages other Linux distribution and software developers to take the time to look at RPM and use it for their own products. Discussion of RPM-related topics and development plans take place on the *redhat-devel-list* mailing list. See Chapter 10, *Frequently Asked Questions*, for subscription information.

RPM Design Goals

A few of the features of RPM are:

- *Upgradability.* With RPM you can upgrade individual components of your system without completely reinstalling. When you buy a new release of Red Hat Linux, you don't need to reinstall your machine (as you do with many other Linux distributions). You instead run an upgrade script that checks to see what packages you have installed, and upgrades those as necessary. Individual configuration files in packages are preserved across upgrades, so you won't lose your customizations.

- *Powerful Querying.* You can search the RPM database for packages or specific files. It is easy to find out what package a file belongs to. The RPM packages are compressed archives, but you can query packages easily and quickly because a binary header is added to the compressed archive and contains all of the information on the package in an uncompressed format.
- *System Verification.* Another feature is verification of packages. If you are worried that you deleted a file important for some package, just verify it. You will be notified of any anomalies. If you find any, you can reinstall the package if necessary. Any configuration files that you modified are preserved during reinstallation.
- *Pristine Sources.* A crucial design goal for RPM was to allow the use of "pristine" software sources, as distributed by the original authors of the software. With RPM, you have the pristine sources along with any patches that we used to compile them. This is a big advantage for several reasons. For one, if a new version of a program comes out, you don't necessarily have to start from scratch to get it to compile under RHCL. You can look at the patch to see what you *might* need to do. All the compiled defaults, and all changes that were made to get the software to build properly on Linux are easily visible this way.

The main requirement to run RPM is Perl 5.x—all of RPM is written in Perl. You must also have working copies of *cpio* and *gzip* in */bin*, which Red Hat Linux includes. Those are the requirements to install packages. To build packages from sources, you also need everything normally required to build software, like *gcc*, *make*, and other development tools.

Using RPM

The most common use of RPM is to install a package:

```
rpm -i foobar-1.0-1.i386.rpm
```

You can even specify the package as an FTP URL, which contains a hostname, directory, and filename:

```
rpm -i ftp://ftp.site.org/RPMS/foobar-1.0-1.i386.rpm
```

The site must allow anonymous FTP access in order for the command to succeed.

Another common use of RPM is to uninstall a package:

```
rpm -u foobar
```

RPM Options

The following paragraphs are a nearly complete description of all the RPM options. For the most complete reference, see the *rpm* man page.

The *query* option is *–q*. A simple use is *rpm –q foobar* which will print the package, version, and release number of the installed foobar package (if it is installed): *foobar–1.0–1*.

Instead of specifying the package name to RPM, you can use the following options with *–q* to specify what you want to query. These are called *Package Specification Options*.

- *–a* queries all currently installed packages.
- *–f* `file` will query the package owning `file`.
- *–F* is the same as *–f* except it takes filenames via *stdin* (i.e., *find /usr/bin* | *rpm –qF*).
- *–p* `packagefile` queries the uninstalled package `packagefile`.
- *–P* is like *–p* except it takes package filenames from *stdin* (i.e., *find /mnt/redhat/redhat–2.0/RPMS* | *rpm –qP*).

There are a number of ways to specify what information to display about queried packages. The following options are used to select the information you are interested in. These are called *Information Selection Options*.

- *–i* displays package information such as name, description, release, size, build date, install date, vendor, and other miscellaneous information.
- *–l* displays the file list for the package (all files that get installed).
- *–s* displays the state of all the files in the package. There are only two possible states, normal and missing.
- *–d* displays a list of files marked as documentation (man pages, information pages, READMEs, etc.).
- *–c* displays a list of files marked as configuration files. These are the files you change after installation to adapt the package to your system (*sendmail.cf*, *passwd*, *inittab*, etc.).

As already mentioned *–i* is used to install packages. The following options can be used when installing a package.

- *–h* gives you feedback as the package installs (much like 'hash' in FTP).
- *–U* does an *upgrade*. After installing the package, any previously installed versions and releases of the same package are uninstalled safely, and your configuration files are preserved.

- *–force* will force an install of a package even though it may conflict with another package that is already installed.
- *–percent* prints "percentage complete" as the package installs (useful for interfacing with other tools, but not really human readable).
- *–test* will tell you if the package would install without conflicting with any packages already installed. The package is *not* actually installed.
- *–search* will search your *rpm search path* (defined in */etc/rpmrc*—read on for details) for the specified package to install.

Use the *–V* to verify a package. A simple use is *rpm –V foobar*, which will verify that all the files in the foobar package are as they were when they were originally installed. This is a useful diagnostic tool when things appear to be broken. You can use any of the *Package Selection Options* listed for querying to specify the packages you wish to verify. For example:

- To verify a package containing a particular file:

```
rpm -Vf /bin/vi
```

- To verify *all* installed packages:

```
rpm -Va
```

- To verify an installed package against an RPM package file:

```
rpm -Vp foobar-1.0-1.rpm
```

Three other main options are:

- *–u* package uninstalls a package.
- *–where* package searches the *rpm search path* for packages matching package, and prints their locations.
- *–b* to build a package (from sources and a spec file). Building packages is not discussed in this book, but you can obtain Red Hat Software's installation guide from them if you are a Linux developer and would like to use RPM for your software.

The following options can be used with any of the above options.

- *–v* print verbose output.
- *–vv* print *very* verbose diagnostic output.

Using RPM Effectively

RPM is a very useful tool for managing your system and diagnosing and fixing problems. The best way to make sense of all the options is to look at some examples.

- Let's say you delete some files by accident, but you aren't sure what you deleted. If you want to verify your entire system and see what might be missing, you would enter:

  ```
  rpm -Va
  ```

  If any of the packages are listed as "bad" you may wish to verify them individually with *–v* for more detailed information:

  ```
  rpm -Vv foobar
  ```

  If some files are missing, or appear to have been corrupted, you should probably either re–install the package or uninstall, then re–install the package.

- Let's say you run across a file that you don't recognize. To find out which package owns it, you would enter:

  ```
  rpm -qf /usr/X11R6/bin/xjewel
  ```

  The output would look like:

  ```
  xjewel-1.6-1
  ```

- We can combine the above two examples in the following scenario. Say you are having problems with */usr/bin/paste*. You would like to verify the package that owns that program but you don't know which package that is. Simply enter:

  ```
  rpm -Vf /usr/bin/paste
  ```

  and the appropriate package will be verified.

- If you are using a program and want to find out more information about it, you can enter the following to find out what documentation came with the package that "owns" that program (in this case *ispell*):

  ```
  rpm -qdf /usr/bin/ispell
  ```

  The output would be:

  ```
  /usr/man/man4/ispell.4
  /usr/man/man4/english.4
  /usr/man/man1/unsq.1
  /usr/man/man1/tryaffix.1
  /usr/man/man1/sq.1
  /usr/man/man1/munchlist.1
  /usr/man/man1/ispell.1
  ```

```
/usr/man/man1/findaffix.1
/usr/man/man1/buildhash.1
/usr/info/ispell.info.gz
/usr/doc/ispell-3.1.18-1/README
```

- You find a new koules RPM, but you don't know what it is. To find out some information on it, enter:

  ```
  rpm -qip koules-1.0-1.i386.rpm
  ```

  The output would be:

  ```
  Name        : koules         Distribution: RHCL 2.0
  Version     : 1.0            Vendor: Red Hat Software
  Release     : 1              Build date: Today
  Install date: <not installed> Build host: daffy.redhat.com
  Group       : Games
  Size        : 403105
  Description : well done SVGAlib game
  ```

- Now you want to see what files the koules RPM installs. You would enter:

  ```
  rpm -qlp koules-1.0-1.i386.rpm
  ```

  The output is:

  ```
  /usr/man/man6/koules.6
  /usr/lib/games/kouleslib/start.raw
  /usr/lib/games/kouleslib/end.raw
  /usr/lib/games/kouleslib/destroy2.raw
  /usr/lib/games/kouleslib/destroy1.raw
  /usr/lib/games/kouleslib/creator2.raw
  /usr/lib/games/kouleslib/creator1.raw
  /usr/lib/games/kouleslib/colize.raw
  /usr/lib/games/kouleslib
  /usr/games/koules
  ```

These are just several examples. As you use the system you will find many more uses for RPM.

RPM Configuration

RPM is configured through the */etc/rpmrc* file. Most of the configuration options are related to building packages, but one is related to installing packages.

A sample configuration file looks like:

```
require_vendor: 1
require_distribution: 1
require_group: 1
distribution: RHCL 2.1
vendor: Red Hat Software
arch_sensitive: 1
topdir: /usr/src/redhat-2.1
```

```
optflags: i386 -O2 -m486
optflags: axp -O
search: /mnt/redhat/RedHat/RPMS
search: /usr/rhs/ftp/pub/redhat-2.0/updates/RPMS
search: ftp://ftp.pht.com/pub/linux/redhat/redhat-2.0/updates/RPMS
```

The *search* lines are used to define a set of search paths for RPM packages. This path is used by the *–search* and *–where* options.

Upgrading

If you have previously installed release 2.0 or later of Red Hat Linux, system upgrades are pretty painless. Otherwise, you must do a complete installation as described in Chapter 3, *Installation in Detail.*

If there is a *README* file on your CD–ROM (or FTP site) please read it. It may contain new or updated information about the upgrade process.

On the CD–ROM is a script called *upgrade.* This is a Perl script that will analyze your installed system and the new Red Hat release, and determine what packages need to be upgraded.

If you haven't done anything strange to your system you can just run the upgrade script as follows:

```
cd /mnt/cdrom
./upgrade RedHat/RPMS/*.rpm
```

If you want to see what *upgrade* does, read on . . .

Running Upgrade in Test Mode

The first thing you should do is run the script in *test mode* as follows:

```
cd /mnt/cdrom
./upgrade -test RedHat/RPMS/*.rpm
```

Running *upgrade* in this mode will *not* actually perform any upgrades—it just tells you what it *would* do during a normal run.

You will first see something like:

```
Red Hat RPM system upgrader, version 0.1
Copyright (c) 1995 Red Hat Software
Finding packages...
Would run: rpm -Uvh rpm-1.4-1.i386.rpm
```

If you are running an older version of RPM than the one listed, the rest of the *./upgrade –test* command may not work properly. If you find that is the case, run the following to upgrade RPM:

```
rpm -Uvh /mnt/cdrom/RedHat/RPMS/rpm-*.i386.rpm
```

After upgrading, you can again enter:

```
./upgrade -test RedHat/RPMS/*.rpm
```

The output of the test mode will continue with something like:

```
Taking stock of things...
Packages installed:  128
Files installed    : 12709
Packages available:  308
Determining packages to upgrade...
Package               New Version          Old Version
===================================================
MAKEDEV               2.2-1                2.1-1
NetKit-A              0.08-4               0.08-2
NetKit-B              0.06-3               0.06-1
SysVinit              2.56-3               2.56-2
...
```

The "Taking stock of things . . . " section can take quite a while as it analyzes your system.

The first list is a list of packages that are new (relative to the packages you have installed on your system already). A second list may be printed that will look similar to:

```
Files moved to                    Version
==========================================
texmf-dvips                       6.1-1
texmf-dvilj                       6.1-1
texmf-latex                       6.1-1
npasswd-dicts                     1.2-2
texmf                             6.1-1
NetKit-B-lpr                      0.06-3
...
```

This is a list of packages that contain files that appear to have moved from other packages. And finally, a third list may be printed:

```
Shared libs moved to              Version
==========================================
ncurses-devel                     1.9.6-1
```

The reason for this list is a little arcane. But in case you want to know, it lists packages that contain *new* versions of *shared* libraries that have been moved from other packages.

After all that, the upgrade script will print a list of commands that *would* be executed if you ran it without the *–test* option.

```
Upgrading packages...
Would run: rpm -Uvh RedHat/RPMS/MAKEDEV-2.2-1.i386.rpm
Would run: rpm -Uvh RedHat/RPMS/NetKit-A-0.08-4.i386.rpm
Would run: rpm -Uvh RedHat/RPMS/NetKit-B-0.06-3.i386.rpm
Would run: rpm -Uvh RedHat/RPMS/NetKit-B-lpr-0.06-3.i386.rpm
Would run: rpm -Uvh RedHat/RPMS/SysVinit-2.56-3.i386.rpm
Would run: rpm -Uvh RedHat/RPMS/XFree86-W32-3.1.2-1.i386.rpm
Would run: rpm -Uvh RedHat/RPMS/Xconfigurator-1.2-1.i386.rpm
Would run: rpm -Uvh RedHat/RPMS/abuse-0.34-2.i386.rpm
...
```

Performing the Upgrade

If you think everything looks right after running the upgrade script in test mode, go ahead and run the script without the *–test* option.

```
cd /mnt/cdrom
./upgrade RedHat/RPMS/*.rpm
```

If you do not agree with what the upgrade script does, you can copy the lines beginning with `Would run: rpm -Uvh ...` to a file, edit it to your liking, and run it as a shell script.

CHAPTER SEVEN

CONTROL-PANEL

The control–panel is a launching pad for a number of different system administration tools. These tools make your life easier by letting you configure things without remembering configuration file formats and awkward command-line options.

To start the control–panel, shown in Figure 7-1, start the X Window System as root with *startx* and type *control–panel* in an xterm. You will need to be root to run the control–panel tools successfully. You can also do this if you already have X running as a normal user. Just type *su –c control–panel* and then type the root password when prompted. If you plan to do other tasks as root, you could type *su* followed by the root password when prompted. You will then be given a root shell. Here, you will need to type *DISPLAY=:0 control–panel &* to get the control panel to work. The `DISPLAY` part tells the control panel to use your display. This syntax works only for a Bourne–compatible shell like bash. If you run tcsh, you would enter *setenv DISPLAY :0; control–panel &*.

Double-clicking on an icon starts up a tool. Please note that you are not prevented from starting two instances of any tool, but doing so is a *very bad idea* because you may try to edit the same files in two places and end up overwriting your own changes. If you do accidentally start a second copy of a tool, you should quit it immediately. Also, do not manually edit any files managed by the control–panel tools while the tools are running. Similarly, do not run any other programs that may change those files while the tools are running.

Figure 7-1. The control-panel

User and Group Configuration

The tool shown in Figure 7-2 manages the users and groups on your system. In a sense, it is a graphical editor for */etc/passwd* and */etc/group*. With this tool you can add and remove users and groups, set login shells, full names, home directories, uid, gids, etc.

RHS Linux User/Group Manager

UserCfg

Name	Passwd	Group	Full Name	Home directory
root	exists	root	root	/root
croot	exists	root	root	/root
bin	locked	bin	bin	/bin
daemon	locked	daemon	daemon	/sbin
adm	locked	adm	adm	/var/adm
lp	locked	lp	lp	/var/spool/lpd
sync	locked	root	sync	/sbin
shutdown	locked	root	shutdown	/sbin
halt	locked	root	halt	/sbin
mail	locked	mail	mail	/var/spool/mail

Add Deactivate Reactivate Remove

Figure 7-2. User and Group Configuration panel

Adding a User

To add a user, click on the `Add` button in the main window. A dialog box will pop up like the one in Figure 7-3 will appear, with some defaults already filled in.

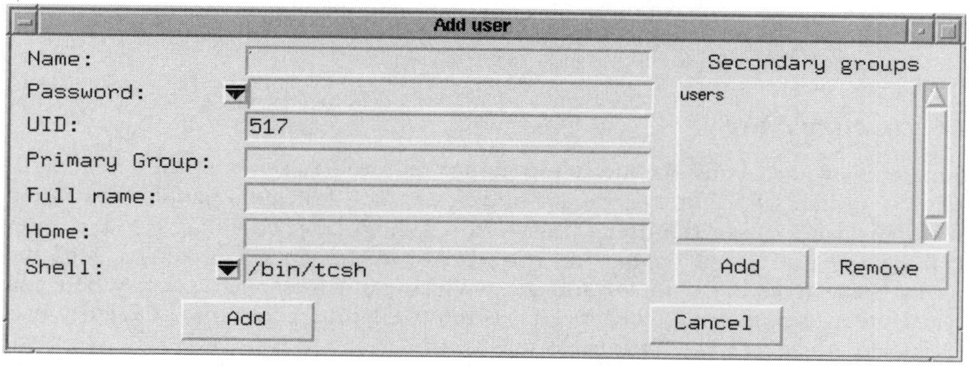

Figure 7–3. Add User Dialog Box

First enter the username. This is *not* the user's first and last name, it is the ID they will use to log on to the system. Do not include any spaces or colons, and do not enter more than eight characters. Press the Enter key when you are finished, and some of the other fields will be filled in with default values. You may change them if you wish, but there is no need to. Next, enter the user's full name, and select a login shell using the drop–down menu. And finally you need to do something with the password. There are three options here, Edit, None, or Lock. None is a very bad option—with no password anyone can log in to your system using this ID. Choosing Lock will prevent anyone from logging in with this ID. Usually you will choose Edit. A small dialog box will appear where you will need to enter a password, and then confirm it by typing it a second time. Click on `Ok` after this, and then click on `Add` in the user entry dialog box to add the user.

If this user does not already have a home directory (and she won't unless you have already created one), you will be asked if you want to create one. Unless you will be mounting home directories from another machine, you should click on `Yes`.

Removing a User

To remove a user, select the user in the main window by clicking on it, and then click on `Remove`. After confirming the removal, you will be asked if you wish to remove the user's home directory and mail spool. You will normally answer `Yes`. After these files are deleted, you will be asked if you want to search the entire filesystem for files that have been "orphaned" by the removal of this user. Orphaned files are those that are not owned by any user in */etc/passwd*. Since you have just removed a user from */etc/passwd* any file that user owned will now be orphaned (except the home directory and mail spool, if you deleted them). If you answer yes, the search will proceed in the background, and all files found will be *chown*ed to `nobody`. To find these files, execute the following command:

```
find / ( -group nobody -o -user nobody ) -print
```

Deactivating a user

Sometimes you may just want to temporarily "remove" a user, with the intention of reinstating him later. The `Deactivate` and `Reactivate` functions handle this. When you deactivate a user, the user's password is locked by prepending a `*` to it, preventing the user from logging in. You also have the option of "collapsing" the user's home directory with *tar* and *gzip*, which can save some space. When you reactivate a user, the password locking is removed, and if the home directory was collapsed, it is expanded back to normal.

Creating a New Group

To create a new group, first switch to group editing mode by selecting `Edit groups` from the menu. Clicking on `Add` brings up a dialog box to specify the group details. First enter a name for the new group. Just like a username, the group name should have no spaces or colons, and should be no longer than eight characters. To add members to the group, click on the `Add` button on the left. A list of usernames will appear from which you can select the group members. When you have selected all the group members, click on `Add`, then click on the lower `Add` button.

File System Configuration

The file system configuration tool shown in Figure 7-4 allows you to easily examine and manipulate filesystem mount points, types, options, etc. It is very useful for manipulating a large number of filesystems. You probably don't want to do this unless you are an experienced system administrator. If you do know what you are doing, it should be fairly straightforward as to how to mount, unmount, and add devices.

The `Reload` entry in the `FSM` menu causes the file system configuration tool to reload */etc/fstab* from your hard drive. If you edit */etc/fstab* by hand while the file system configuration tool is running (which you shouldn't do), you probably want to reload.

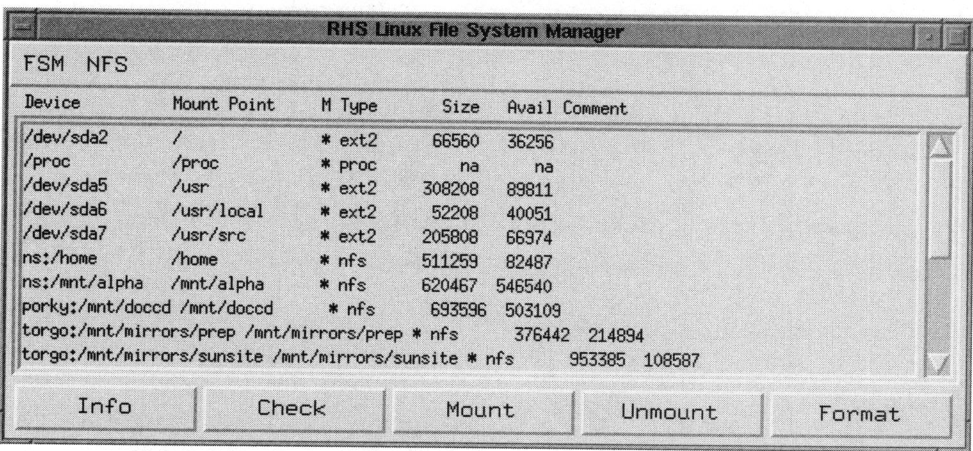

Figure 7-4. File System Configuration panel

To use the buttons along the bottom of the window, select a filesystem in the main window, and click on one of the buttons. The buttons perform the following functions:

- *Info.* Displays information on the filesystem, including the device, partition type, filesystem type, mount point and options, comment, size, percent used.
- *Check.* Performs a filesystem check (*fsck*) on the partition. You can only do this on *unmounted* partitions—if the partition is mounted, you will get an error and you will have to unmount it first.
- *Mount.* Mounts the selected filesystem.
- *Unmount.* Unmounts the selected filesystem.
- *Format.* Creates a new filesystem on the selected partition. This will erase all data on the selected partition! You can only do this on *unmounted* partitions—if the partition is mounted, you will get an error and you will have to unmount it first.
- *Edit.* Brings up a dialog box where you can edit the mount point, mount options, comment, etc.

Adding NFS Mounts

To mount a filesystem via NFS, select `Add Mount` from the `NFS` menu. A dialog box will appear and you will have to fill in the following values:

- *Device.* Enter the hostname and path, separated by a colon. For example, `foo.bar.com:/usr/exported` indicates the */usr/exported* directory on **foo.bar.com**.

- *Mount Point.* Enter the directory on your machine where you want to mount the NFS filesystem. For example, */mnt/foo.*
- *Options.* Enter the mount options for this filesystem. The default is `soft,intr,rw`. The `rw` means is read–write, and `soft,intr` are options that make your system a little more resilient when the remote server goes down. See the *mount* man page for a complete list of available options.
- *Comment.* This optional field can be used to store a small comment.

After filling everything out properly, click on `OK`. At this point the entry is made in your */etc/fstab*, but the filesystem is not actually mounted. To mount it, select it in the main window and click on `Mount`.

Printer Configuration

The printer configuration tool maintains */etc/printcap*, print spool directories, and print filters. The filters are designed to use GhostScript (*gs*) and *nenscript* to allow you to print plain text as well as PostScript files.

While configuring your printers, keep in mind that *lpr* prints to the printer named *lp* by default. You will probably want *lp* to be one of your printer queue names.

Needless to say, ghostscript and nenscript should be installed.

To add a new printer, click on `Add`. This will bring up a dialog box where you indicate if you are adding a remote printer, or a local one. If your printer is connected to your machine's parallel or serial port select local; if it is somewhere on the network select remote.

For a local printer, you need to fill in the following values:

- *Names.* Enter the names you want to give to this printer (queue). You can have multiple names, separated by a `|` character, for example, `lp|lp0|PostScript`.
- *Spool Directory.* Enter a unique directory to hold documents queued for printing on this printer. For example, */var/spool/lpd/lp0.*
- *File Limit.* If you want to limit the size of documents printed, enter a size in KB here. A 0 indicates no limit.
- *Printer Device.* This is the physical device to which your printer is connected. For example, */dev/lp1.*
- *Input Filter.* If you have a custom filter, enter the filename (full path) here. Otherwise, you should click on `Select`. This will bring up a dialog box where you select your `Printer Type`, `Resolution`, `Paper Size`, and you indicate if your printer requires an `EOF` character to be sent to it at the end of each job (many printers used under DOS require this).

- *Suppress Headers.* If you select this, no header pages will be printed for each job.

For a remote printer, you will fill in the following values:

- *Names.* See local printer.
- *Spool Directory.* See local printer.
- *File Limit.* See local printer.
- *Remote Host.* Enter the hostname of the machine that has the printer. For example, **printer.foo.com**.
- *Remote Queue.* Enter the name of the queue on the remote machine for the remote printer. For example, `PostScript`.

Click on `Ok` and your new printer is added. Some versions of the *lpd* printer daemon may need to be restarted before they will recognize the new printer. To do this select `Restart lpd` from the `lpd` menu.

Network Configuration

The network configuration panel shown in Figure 7-5 is designed to allow easy manipulation of parameters such as IP address, gateway address, network address, etc., as well as name servers and */etc/hosts.* Network devices can be added, removed, configured, brought up, brought down, etc. Ethernet, loopback and SLIP devices are supported, although SLIP support should be considered experimental.

Adding an Ethernet Device

If you have added an Ethernet card to your machine since you installed, or you didn't set up your Ethernet card at install time, you can configure it by clicking on `Add` in the `Interfaces` panel. This will bring up a window where you need to click on `ethernet` and enter a device name. The device name should be something like `eth0`, or `eth1` if this is your second Ethernet device. Click on `OK` after doing this.

In the next window you have to fill in the following parameters:

- *Ethernet Device.* This is already filled in—it is the device you entered in the previous window.
- *IP Address.* Enter an IP address for your Ethernet device.
- *Netmask.* Enter the network mask for your Ethernet.
- *Network.* Enter the network address for your Ethernet.
- *Broadcast.* Enter the broadcast address for your Ethernet.

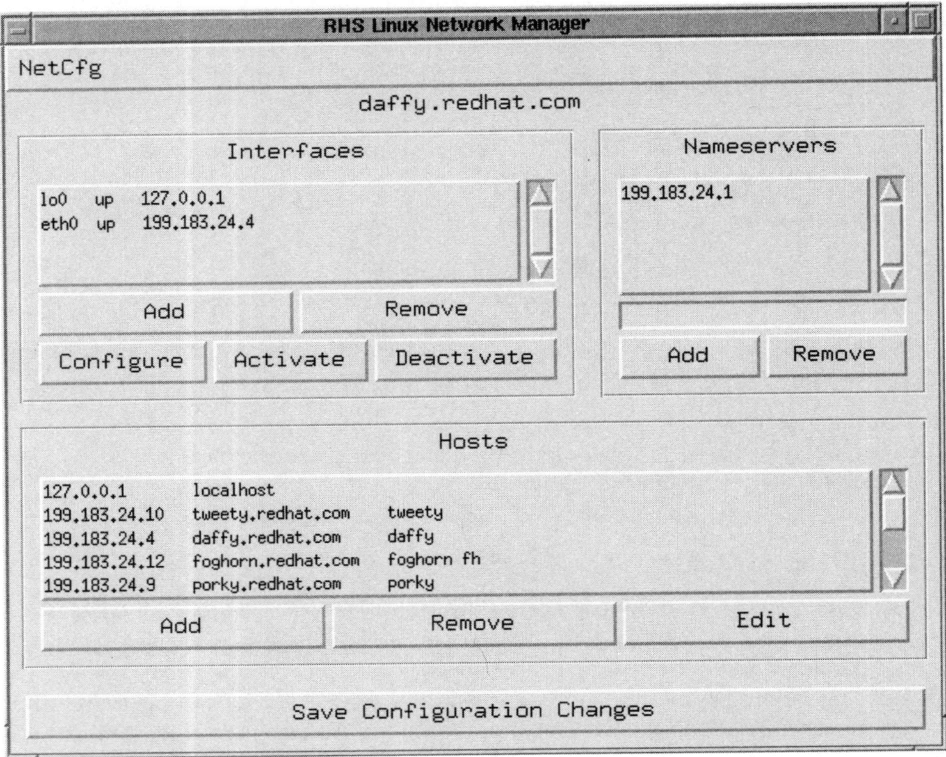

Figure 7-5. Network Configuration panel

- *Gateway.* If you have a gateway, enter its IP address here. If you don't have a gateway, enter `none`.
- *Activate at Boot.* If you want the device to be configured automatically when your machine boots (usually a good idea), select this by clicking on the box.

After filling everything in, click on `OK`. The device should then appear in your `Interfaces` list, but it is not currently active (it says "down"). To activate it click on `Activate`. If it does not come up properly, you may need to reconfigure it by clicking on `Configure`.

Adding a SLIP or PPP Device

To configure SLIP or PPP for your machine, click on `Add` in the `Interfaces` panel. This will bring up a window where you need to click on `slip` or `ppp` and enter a device name. The device name should be something like `sl0` or `ppp0`, *not* your modem device. Click on `OK` after doing this.

In the next window you have to fill in the following parameters (these are for SLIP—PPP is similar):

- *SLIP Device.* This is already filled in—it is the device you entered in the previous window.
- *Local IP Address.* Enter an IP address for your machine's SLIP device. Leave this blank if your ISP uses dynamic addressing (this will require that you edit */etc/dip-script* to comment out the `get $local` line).
- *DIP Script.* You should enter */etc/dip-script*, unless you want to make a custom script, or have more than one SLIP or PPP device.
- *Remote IP Address.* Enter the IP address of the machine you are connecting to.
- *Modem Speed.* Enter your modem speed (e.g., `38400`).
- *Phone Number.* Enter the phone number to call up the remote machine.
- *Login Name.* Enter the name with which to log in to the remote machine.
- *Password.* Enter the password you need to log in to the remote machine.
- *Connect String.* Enter the string your modem sends when the connection is made (e.g., `ing . . .`).
- *Connection Type.* Enter the type of connection you want to make. For a SLIP device this is either `SLIP` or `CSLIP` (for a PPP device use `PPP`).
- *Activate at Boot.* If you want the device to be configured automatically when your machine boots select this by clicking on the box.
- *Restart.* If you select this a small script will be executed that watches the connection to make sure it is active. If the connection goes down, the script will try to re-establish it.

After filling everything in, click on `OK`. The device should then appear in your `Interfaces` list, but it is not currently active (it says "down"). To activate it click on `Activate`. If it does not come up properly, you may need to reconfigure it by clicking on `Configure`.

It is likely that you will have to edit */etc/dip-script* a little to get everything to work. Unfortunately there is no way to automate this. You simply need to adjust it to talk to your SLIP or PPP server in the manner it expects. The things to pay attention to are the `wait` lines, which must recognize stuff your server returns.

Do not edit the `@@@......@@@` entries—those are automatically filled in with the values you just entered while configuring the device.

Time and Date

The time machine allows you to change the time and date by clicking on the appropriate part of the time and date display and clicking on the arrows to change the value.

The system clock is not changed until you click on the Set System Clock button.

Click on Reset Time to set the time machine time back to that of the system.

CAUTION: Changing the time can seriously confuse programs that depend on the normal progression of time, and could possibly cause problems. Try to quit as many applications and processes as possible before changing the time or date.

CHAPTER EIGHT

SYSTEM ADMINISTRATION

This chapter is an overview of the RHC Linux system. It will illustrate things that you may not know about the system and things that are somewhat different from other UNIX systems. Note that most system administration tasks are performed with the control–panel, which is covered in Chapter 7, *Control-Panel.*

Filesystem Structure

Red Hat Software is committed to the Linux File System Standard, a collaborative document that defines the names and locations of many files and directories. We will continue to track the standard to keep Red Hat compliant.

While compliance with the standard means many things, the two most important are compatibility with other compliant systems, and the ability to mount the */usr* partition as read–only. The */usr* partition contains common executables and is not meant to be changed by users. Because of this, the */usr* partition can be mounted from the CD–ROM or from another machine via read–only NFS. The current FSSTND standard document is the authoritative reference to any FSSTND compliant filesystem, but the standard leaves many areas undefined or extensible. In this section we provide an overview of the standard and a description of the parts of the filesystem not covered by the standard.

The complete standard can be viewed at *http://www.eg.bucknell.edu/~quinlan/fsstnd.*

Overview of the FSSTND

The directories and files noted here are a small subset of those specified by the FSSTND document. Check the latest FSSTND document for the most up-to-date and complete information.

The /etc directory

The */etc* directory, shown in Figure 8-1, is reserved for configuration files that are local to your machine. No binaries are put in */etc* (binaries that were put in */etc* in the past should now go into */sbin*, or possibly */bin*).

The *X11* and *skel* directories should be subdirectories of */etc*.

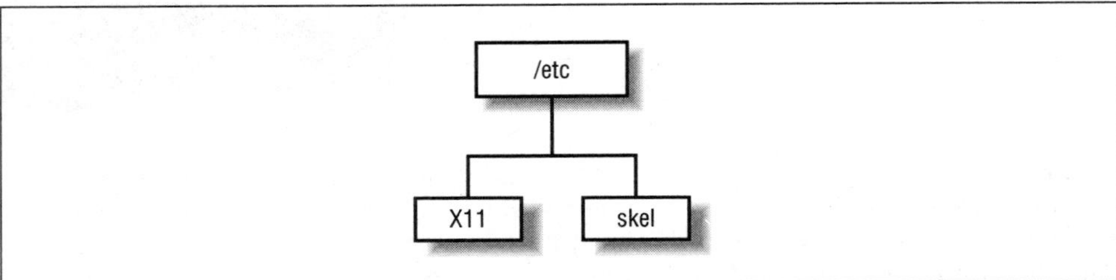

Figure 8–1. /etc directory

The *X11* directory is for X11 configuration files such as *XF86Config*. The *skel* directory is for "skeleton" user files, which are files used to populate a HOME directory when a user is first created.

The /lib directory

The */lib* directory should contain only those libraries that are needed to execute the binaries in */bin* and */sbin*.

The /sbin directory

The */sbin* directory is for executables used only by the root user, and only those executables needed to boot and mount */usr* and perform system recovery operations. The FSSTND says:

> */sbin* typically contains files essential for booting the system in addition to the binaries in */bin*. Anything executed after */usr* is known to be mounted (when there are no problems) should be placed in */usr/sbin*. Local–only system administration binaries should be placed into */usr/local/sbin*.

At a minimum, the following programs should be in */sbin*:

`clock, getty, init, update, mkswap, swapon, swapoff, halt, reboot, shutdown, fdisk, fsck.*, mkfs.*, lilo, arp, ifconfig, route`

The /usr directory

The */usr* directory is for files that are shareable across a whole site. The */usr* directory usually has its own partition, and it should be mountable as read-only. Figure 8-2 shows the subdirectories of */usr*.

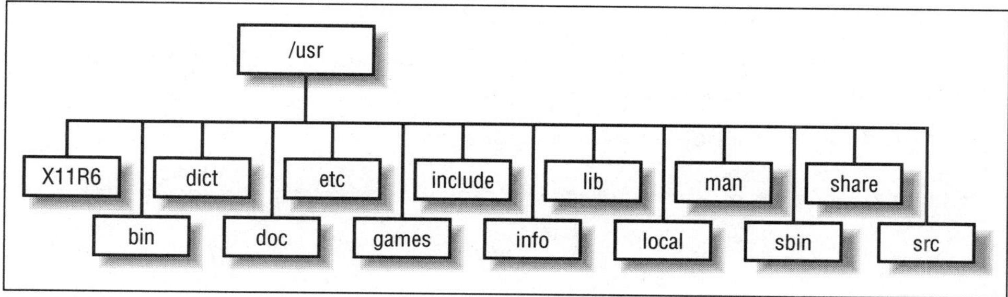

Figure 8–2. /usr directory

The *X11R6* directory is for the X Window System (XFree86 on RHC Linux); *bin* is for executables; *doc* is for random non–man page documentation; *etc* is for site–wide configuration files; *include* is for C header files; *info* is for GNU information files; *lib* is for libraries; *man* is for man pages; *sbin* is for system administration binaries (those that do not belong in */sbin*); and *src* is for source code.

The /usr/local directory

The FSSTND says:

> The */usr/local* hierarchy is for use by the system administrator when installing software locally. It needs to be safe from being overwritten when the system software is updated. It may be used for programs and data that are shareable amongst a group of machines, but not found in */usr*.

The */usr/local* directory is similar in structure to the */usr* directory. It has the subdirectories shown in Figure 8-3, which are similar in purpose to those in the */usr* directory.

The /var directory

Since the FSSTND requires that you be able to mount */usr* as read–only, any programs that write log files or need spool or lock directories probably should write them to the */var* directory. The FSSTND says */var* is for:

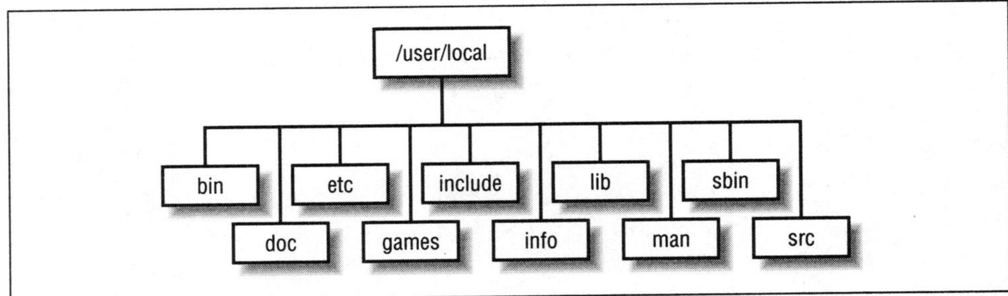

Figure 8-3. /usr/local directory

> ...variable data files. This includes spool directories and files, administrative and logging data, and transient and temporary files.

Figure 8-4 shows the subdirectory tree under */var*.

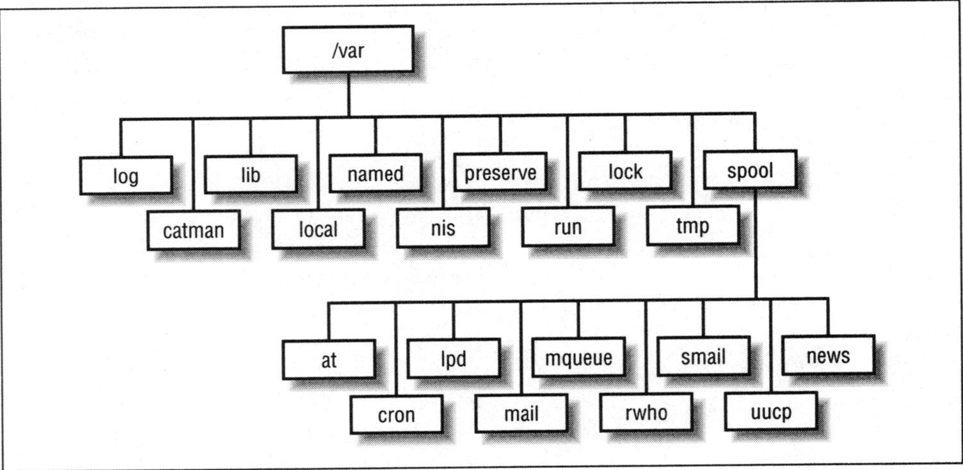

Figure 8-4. /var directory

System log files such as *wtmp* and *lastlog* go in */var/log*. The */var/lib* directory also contains the RPM system databases. Formatted man pages go in */var/catman*, and lock files go in */var/lock*. The */var/spool* directory has subdirectories for various systems that need to store data files.

/usr/local

In RHC Linux, the intended use for */usr/local* is slightly different from that specified by the FSSTND. The FSSTND says that */usr/local* should be where you store software that is to remain safe from system software upgrades. Since system upgrades from RHS are done safely with the RPM system and Glint, you don't need to protect files by putting them in */usr/local*. Instead, we recommend you use */usr/local* for software that is local to your machine.

For instance, let's say you have mounted */usr* via read–only NFS from *beavis*. If there is a package or program you would like to install, but are not allowed to write to *beavis*, you should install it under */usr/local*. Later perhaps, if you've managed to convince the system administrator of *beavis* to install the program on */usr*, you can uninstall it from */usr/local*.

Special Red Hat File Locations

In addition to the files pertaining to the RPM system that reside in */var/lib/rpm* (see Chapter 6, *Package Management with RPM*), there are two other special locations that are reserved for RHC Linux configuration and operation.

The control–panel and related tools put lots of stuff in */usr/lib/rhs*. There is probably nothing here that you would want to edit. It is mostly small scripts, bitmaps and text files.

The other location, */etc/sysconfig*, stores configuration information. The major users of the files in this directory are the scripts that run at boot time. It is possible to edit these by hand, but it would be better to use the proper control–panel tool.

Users, Groups, and User-Private Groups

Managing users and groups has traditionally been tedious. RHC Linux has a few tools and conventions that make users and groups easier to manage, and more useful.

The easiest way to manage users and groups is through the Users and Groups module of the control–panel (see Chapter 7 for details on the control–panel and the section called "User and Group Configuration" for details on the Users and Groups module).

You can also use *adduser* to create a new user from the command line.

Standard Users

Table 8-1 lists the standard users set up by the installation process (this is essentially the */etc/passwd* file). The group ID (GID) in this table is the *primary group* for the user. See the section called "User Private Groups" for details on how groups are used.

Table 8-1: Standard Users

User	UID	GID	HOME Directory	Shell
root	0	0	/root	/bin/bash
bin	1	1	/bin	
daemon	2	2	/sbin	
adm	3	4	/var/adm	
lp	4	7	/var/spool/lpd	
sync	5	0	/sbin	/bin/sync
shutdown	6	0	/sbin	/sbin/shutdown
halt	7	0	/sbin	/sbin/halt
mail	8	12	/var/spool/mail	
news	9	13	/var/spool/news	
uucp	10	14	/var/spool/uucp	
operator	11	0	/root	/bin/bash
games	12	100	/usr/local/games	
gopher	13	30	/usr/lib/gopher-data	
ftp	14	50	/usr/rhs/ftp	
nobody	99	99	/root	

Standard Groups

Table 8-2 lists the standard groups as set up by the installation process (this is essentially the */etc/group* file).

Table 8-2: Standard Groups

Group	Group ID	Members
root	0	root
bin	1	root,bin,daemon
daemon	2	root,bin,daemon
sys	3	root,bin,adm
adm	4	root,adm,daemon
tty	5	
disk	6	root
lp	7	daemon,lp
mem	8	
kmem	9	
wheel	10	root
mail	12	mail
news	13	news
uucp	14	uucp

Table 8-2: Standard Groups (continued)

Group	Group ID	Members
man	15	
games	20	
gopher	30	
dip	40	
ftp	50	ftp
nobody	99	
users	100	

User Private Groups

RHC Linux uses a user private group (UPG) scheme, which makes UNIX groups much easier to use. The UPG scheme does not add or change anything in the standard UNIX way of handling groups. It simply offers a new convention for handling groups. Whenever you create a new user, by default, he or she has a unique group. The scheme works as follows:

- *User Private Group*. Each user has its own primary group, to which only it is a member.
- *umask = 002*. The traditional UNIX umask is 022, which prevents other users *and other members of a user's primary group* from modifying a user's files. Since every user has his own private group in the UPG scheme, this "group protection" is not needed. A umask of 002 will prevent users from modifying other users' private files. The umask is set in */etc/profile.*
- *SGID bit on Directories*. By setting the SGID bit on a directory (with `chmod g+s` *`directory`*), files created in that directory will have their group set to the directory's group.

Most computing sites like to create a group for each major project and assign people to the groups they need to be in. Managing files traditionally has been difficult, though, because when someone creates a file it is owned by the primary group he or she belongs to. When a single person works on multiple projects, it becomes hard to make the files owned by the group that is associated with that project. The UPG scheme is a system in which groups are automatically assigned to files on a project-by-project basis, which makes managing group projects very simple.

Let's say you have a big project called *devel*, with many people editing the devel files in a *devel* directory. Make a group called `devel`, *chgrp* the *devel* directory to *devel*, and add the all the devel users to the `devel` group. Now, all the devel users will be able to edit the devel files and create new files in the *devel* directory, and these files will always retain their `devel` group. Thus, they will always be editable by other devel users.

If you have multiple projects like *devel*, and users who are working on multiple projects, these users will never have to change their umask or group when they move from project to project. The SGID bit on each project's main directory "selects" the proper group.

Since each user's HOME directory is owned by the user and their private group, it is safe to set the SGID bit on the HOME directory. However, by default, files are created with the primary group of the user, so the SGID bit would be redundant.

User private group rationale

Since the UPG scheme is new, many people have questions about it, and they wonder why it is necessary. The following is the rationale for the scheme.

You'd like to have a group of people work on a set of files in, say, the */usr/lib/emacs/site–lisp* directory. You trust a few people to mess around in there, but certainly not everyone. So you enter:

```
chown -R root.emacs /usr/lib/emacs/site-lisp
```

and you add the proper users to the group.

To allow the users to actually create files in the directory you enter:

```
chmod 775 /usr/lib/emacs/site-lisp
```

But when a user creates a new file it gets the group of the users default group (usually *users*). To prevent this you enter:

```
chmod 2775 /usr/lib/emacs/site-lisp
```

which causes everything in the directory to get created with the "emacs" group.

But the new file needs to be mode 664 for another user in the emacs group to be able to edit it. To do this you make the default umask 002.

Well, this all works fine, except that if your default group is `users`, every file you create in your home directory will be writable by everybody in `users` (usually everyone). To fix this, you make each user have a "private group" as their default group.

At this point, by making the default umask 002 and giving everyone a private default group, you can easily set up groups that users can take advantage of without doing any magic. Just create the group, add the users, and do the above chown and chmod on the group's directories.

The Boot Process, Init, and Shutdown

RHC Linux uses System V style *init* scripts (scripts that run at boot time), which live in */etc/rc.d*. These scripts take care of initializing networking, *nfs*, *cron*, *syslog*, *sendmail*, *lpd*, etc. You should *not* mess around with these files unless you are an experienced system administrator—you could easily prevent your system from booting.

System V Init

System V *init* is becoming the standard in the Linux world to control the startup of software at boot time because it is easier to use, more powerful, and more flexible than the traditional BSD *init*.

The *init* binary is located in */sbin* and not */etc*. This is important if you try and upgrade a machine to System V *init* without re–installing and reformatting. The linux kernel looks in */etc* for its *init* first, so you may need to delete your old *init*, if any.

SYSV *init* config files are in a subdirectory of */etc* instead of residing directly in */etc*, as in BSD *init*. This directory is called *rc.d*. In there you will find *rc.sysinit* and the following directories:

```
init.d
rc0.d
rc1.d
rc2.d
rc3.d
rc4.d
rc5.d
rc6.d
```

init.d contains a bunch of scripts. You need one script for each service you need to start at boot time or when changing runlevels. Services include things like networking, *nfs*, *sendmail*, *httpd*, etc. Services do not include things like *setserial* that must only be run once and then exited. Things like that should go in *rc.local*.

rc.local should be in */etc/rc.d*. Most systems include one even though it doesn't do much. You can also include an *rc.serial* in */etc/rc.d* if you need to do serial port specific things at boot time.

The chain of events is as follows:

1. The kernel looks in several places for *init* and runs the first one it finds
2. *init* runs */etc/rc.d/rc.sysinit*
3. *rc.sysinit* does a bunch of things and then runs *rc.serial* (if it exists)

4. *init* runs *rc.local*
5. *init* runs all the scripts for the default run level

The default run level is specified in */etc/inittab*. You should have a line close to the top like:

```
id:3:initdefault:
```

From this, you'd look in the second column and see that the default runlevel is 3, as should be the case for most systems. If you want to change it, you can edit */etc/inittab* by hand and change the 3. Be very careful when you are messing with the *inittab*. If you do mess up though, you can get in to fix it by rebooting and doing:

```
LILO boot: linux single
```

This should allow you to boot into single user mode so you can fix it.

Now, how does it run all the right scripts? If you do an *ls –l* on *rc3.d*, you might see something like:

```
lrwxrwxrwx 1 root root 17  13:11 S10network -> ../init.d/network
lrwxrwxrwx 1 root root 16  13:11 S30syslog -> ../init.d/syslog
lrwxrwxrwx 1 root root 14  13:32 S40cron -> ../init.d/cron
lrwxrwxrwx 1 root root 14  13:11 S50inet -> ../init.d/inet
lrwxrwxrwx 1 root root 13  13:11 S60nfs -> ../init.d/nfs
lrwxrwxrwx 1 root root 15  13:11 S70nfsfs -> ../init.d/nfsfs
lrwxrwxrwx 1 root root 18  13:11 S75keytable -> ../init.d/keytable
lrwxrwxrwx 1 root root 23  13:11 S80sendmail -> ../init.d/sendmail.init
lrwxrwxrwx 1 root root 18  13:11 S90lpd -> ../init.d/lpd.init
lrwxrwxrwx 1 root root 11  13:11 S99local -> ../rc.local
```

Notice that there are no real "files" in the directory. Everything there is a link to one of the scripts in the *init.d* directory. The links also have an `S` and a number at the beginning. The `S` means to start this particular script and a `K` would mean to stop it. The number is just there for ordering purposes. *init* will start all the services based on the order they appear. You can duplicate numbers, but it will only confuse you somewhat. You need to use two digit numbers, along with an uppercase `S` or `K` to start or stop the services you need to.

How does it start and stop services? Each of the scripts accepts an argument that can be `start` or `stop`. You can execute those scripts by hand with a command like:

```
/etc/rc.d/init.d/httpd.init stop
```

to stop the httpd server. *init* just reads the name and if it has a `K`, it calls the script with the `stop` argument. If it has an `S` it calls the script with a `start` argument.

Why all these runlevels?

Some people want an easy way to set up machines to be multipurpose. I could have a "server" runlevel that just runs *httpd*, *sendmail*, networking, etc. Then I could have a "user" runlevel that runs *xdm*, networking, etc.

Red Hat Runlevels

Generally, RHC Linux runs in run level 3—full multiuser mode. The following runlevels are used in RHC Linux:

- *0* Halt
- *1* Single user mode
- *2* Multiuser mode, without NFS
- *3* Full multiuser mode
- *6* Reboot

If your machine gets into a state where it will not boot due to a bad */etc/inittab*, or will not let you log in because you have screwed up */etc/passwd* or simply forgotten your password, boot into single user mode by typing *linux 1* at the LILO boot prompt. A very bare system will come up and you will be given a shell from which you can fix things.

Shutting Down the System

To shut down RHC Linux, issue the *shutdown* command. You can read the shutdown man page for complete details, but the two most common usages are:

```
shutdown -h now
shutdown -r now
```

They will each cleanly shut down the system. After shutting everything down, the first will halt the machine, and the second will reboot.

Avoid running the *reboot* or *halt* commands directly.

CHAPTER NINE

GLINT

Red Hat provides a graphical tool to aid in package installation and removal. It's called glint (Graphical Linux INstallation Tool) and runs under the X Window System. It allows easy installation, uninstallation, upgrading, querying, and verification of packages. The interface is similar to the one found in many popular file managers and should be simple to use.

Operations are performed in glint by selecting the packages to operate on and then selecting the operation to perform via pushbuttons. Installing a package places all of the components of that package on your system. Uninstalling one removes all traces of the package except for configuration files you have modified. Upgrading a package installs the newly available version and uninstalls all other versions that were previously installed. This allows quick upgrading to the latest releases of packages.

The query operation lets you examine the details of both installed or available packages. You can view the description of the package, where and when it was built, the files in the package, and other attributes. All of the configuration and documentation components of each package are clearly marked as such to reduce the time you spend looking for them.

Using glint to perform all of these operations is the same as using RPM to do them from the command line. However, the graphical nature of glint often makes these operations easier to perform.

Starting glint

To start glint, simply run *glint &* from any X terminal window. That will bring up a window that looks like the one in Figure 9-1. Any user can use glint to query and verify packages, but if you need to install, uninstall, or upgrade packages be sure to run glint as root.

There are two main parts to the glint interface. The first, on the left, allows you to browse and select the packages installed on your system. The right side contains buttons that manipulate the selected packages.

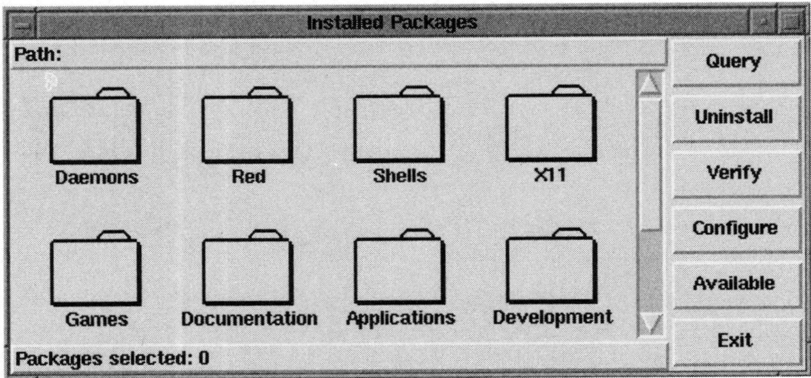

Figure 9–1. Main glint window

The Package Display

Each folder icon in glint represents a group of packages. Each group can contain other groups, which allows for flexible locations of packages. Groups are used to place packages that perform similar functions in similar locations. For example, Red Hat includes many application programs such as editors and spreadsheets. All of the text–based ones appear in the "Applications" group. Inside of that group, there is another grouping for all of the editors that are shipped.

By convention, groups are written in the same way as UNIX paths. The top-most group is written first, and subsequent groups follow with a slash separating the group names. This means that an X–based drawing program appears in the X11/Applications/Graphics group.

To view the packages and subgroups within a group, double-click the left mouse button on a group's folder icon. The window will then change to show what that package contains. The top line of the package display shows which group you're currently looking in, as well as the groups leading to the current one. To return to the previous group you were looking at, double-click on the `Back` folder, which is always in the upper left hand corner of the folder area (though it often gets scrolled away).

If you'd like to examine a subgroup in a new window, double-click the middle mouse button on its folder. If your mouse has only two buttons, click both. This will create a new window with that group in it.

Context Sensitive Menus

Pressing the right mouse button on any icon in the package window brings up a small, *context sensitive* menu. The exact items it contains depend on where you press it. They all contain options to select or deselect the item, and many let you install, uninstall, query, upgrade, or verify the item you clicked on. There's more information on how to do these things later in this chapter.

To choose an item from a context sensitive menu, press and hold the right mouse button on a icon. While still holding the right button down, move the mouse pointer over the item you'd like to select (which will then be highlighted). Release the right mouse button to select that item and make the menu disappear.

Selecting Packages

To select a single package, click the left mouse button on it. You'll notice a thin border appear around the package's icon (as shown in Figure 9-2) that shows that it's currently selected. To unselect it, click the left mouse button on it and the border will disappear. The number of packages currently selected is always displayed at the bottom of the window. A group's folder icon displays the number of packages inside of that group that have been selected, or `All` if all of them have been.

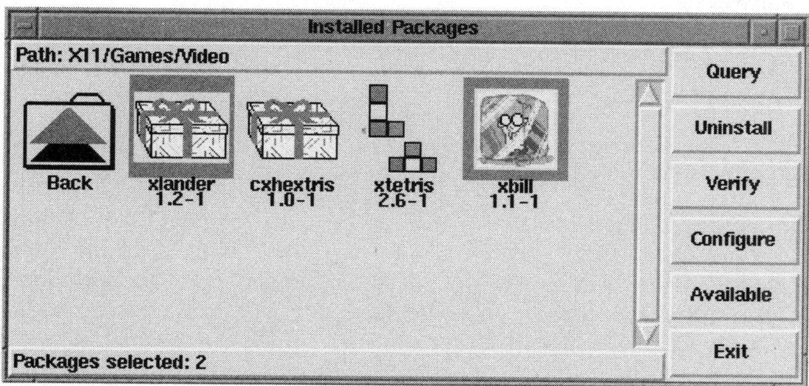

Figure 9–2. Selecting packages in glint

The context sensitive menu for a package also allows easy selection and unselection. Using the `select` and `unselect` options on a package's icon selects or unselects that package, while those options on a group's folder icon select and unselect all of the packages in that group. Using these menu options makes selecting groups of packages much quicker then selecting each package individually.

Viewing Available Packages

To see what packages are available for you to install, choose the `Available` push-button from any glint window. After a few moments, a new window, like the one shown in Figure 9-3, will appear. The differences in the title and buttons indicate that this window is listing packages you may install. Navigating through these packages and selecting them is the same as in the other glint windows.

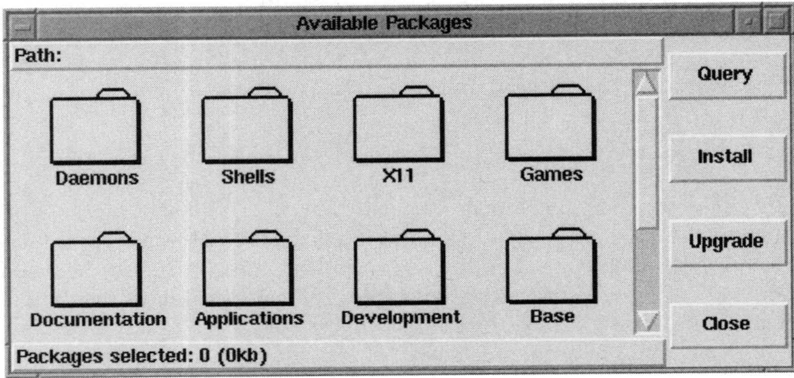

Figure 9-3. Available window

If you get an error message from glint saying that it can't find any RPMs, see the section below on Configuration.

Configuration

The only configuration information glint needs is the path to new RPMs. When you're using your Red Hat Linux CD-ROM, this will probably be */mnt/cdrom/RedHat/RPMS*, which is the default path for glint. If you download new RPMs from the Internet or want to install RPMs via a NFS mounted CD-ROM this path will probably be different for you.

To change this path, first be sure to close all of the windows listing available packages you may have open. Then choose the `Configuration` option from one of the remaining windows. This will open a dialog box like the one shown in Figure 9-4. Here you can type the full path to the RPMs you'd like to look at. Choosing the `Save` button will save this path, making it the default for future glint sessions. The `Default` button restores the path to the one that glint used when it started.

After changing this path and closing the dialog box, you can use the `Available` button to view the packages available in the new location.

Figure 9–4. Configuration window

Package Manipulation

Once a package has been installed, there are several maintenance operations you can perform on it. These include querying, verifying, and uninstalling existing packages, and installing and upgrading new packages.

Querying Packages

The easiest way to query a single package or group is to use the query option from the icon's context sensitive menu. If you want to query a more diverse set of packages, select them all and use the `Query` button in one of the windows.

Using either of these methods creates a window like the one shown in Figure 9-5. If you choose only one package, it will look a bit different however, so some of this won't apply.

On the very left of the window is a list of the packages that have been queried. Selecting one of them will change the information in the rest of the window. You may step through them in order by using the `Next` and `Previous` buttons on the right side of the window.

The name, version, and release of the current package are in the top middle of the query window. Immediately below this is the description of the package, which can be quite large. A scroll bar is there to let you read the whole thing.

Below the description is a list of the files contained in the package. Along with the full path to the file, the file list tells you a couple of other things. If a `D` appears to the left of the path, that file is a documentation file and would be a good thing to read. If a `C` appears there, then the file is a configuration file. A `*` means that the correct version of that file is not installed on your system. This can occur because a more recent version of a package was installed or two packages contain different versions of the same file.

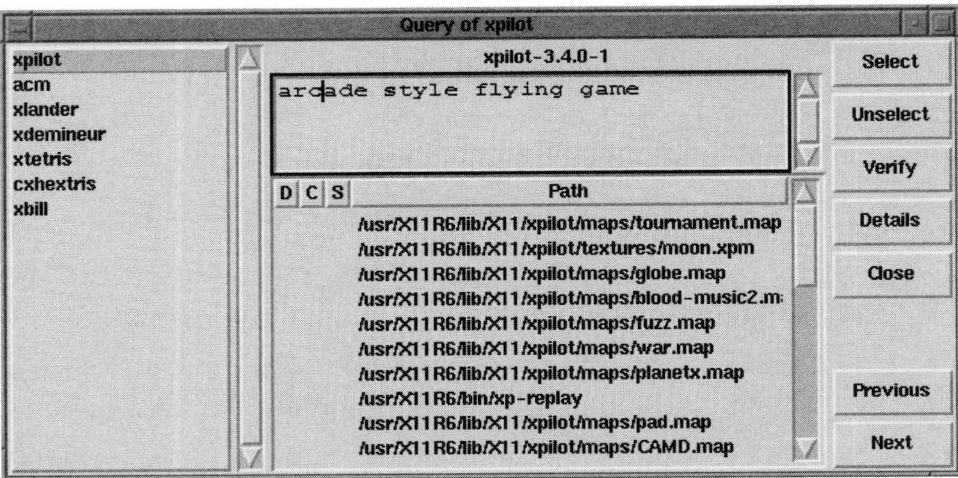

Figure 9–5. Query window

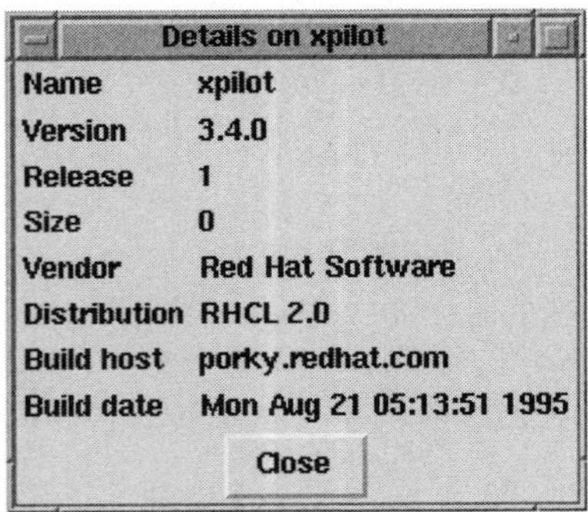

Figure 9–6. Query details

More information on a package can be seen by clicking on the `Details` pushbutton. A window like the one in Figure 9-6 will then appear. This lists more information about the package being displayed in the main query window. When you select a new package in the query window, the information in the details window will change to reflect your new choice.

You may also select, unselect, or verify a package while querying it by using the buttons provided. Click on the `Close` button when you are finished looking at the packages.

Verifying Packages

Verifying a package checks all of the files in the package to ensure they match the ones present on your system. The checksum, file size, permissions, and owner attributes are all checked against the database. This check can be used when you suspect that one of program files has become corrupted due to the installation of new programs.

Choosing the packages to verify is the same as choosing the packages to query. Select the packages and use the `Verify` button or choose the `Verify` entry from a context sensitive menu. A window opens like the one in Figure 9-7.

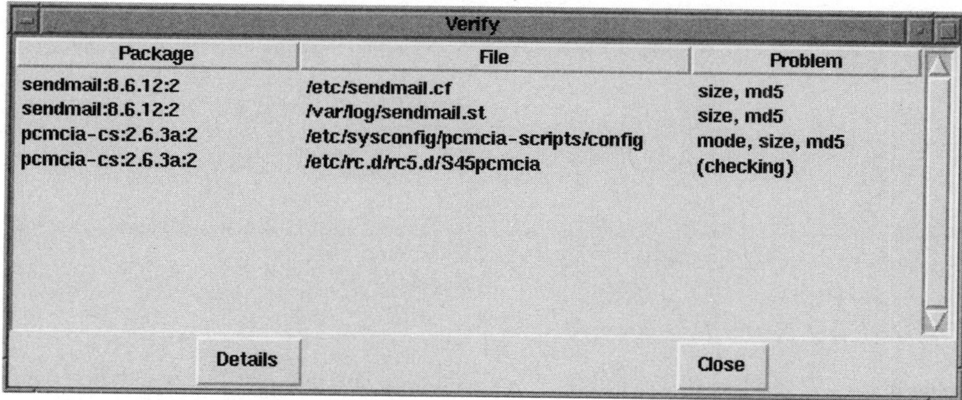

Figure 9-7. Verify window

The three columns in this window describe the package with a problem in it, the file that has the problem, and a brief description of the discrepancies that were found. While the check is running, the current file being checked appears as the last element in the list, and the problem is listed as `(checking)`. A full list of the problems that can be found through verification appears in Table 9-1.

Table 9-1: Possible Problems Found by Verification

Problem	Description
missing	The file is no longer on your system
mode	Permission bits have changed
size	File's size has changed
uid	Owner's UID has changed
gid	Owner's GID has changed
md5	The md5 checksum has changed
link	The file is a symlink to the wrong place

To get more information on the problems found with a file, double-click on the file's path. A window like the one shown in Figure 9-8 lists the expected and current values of the attributes that are amiss.

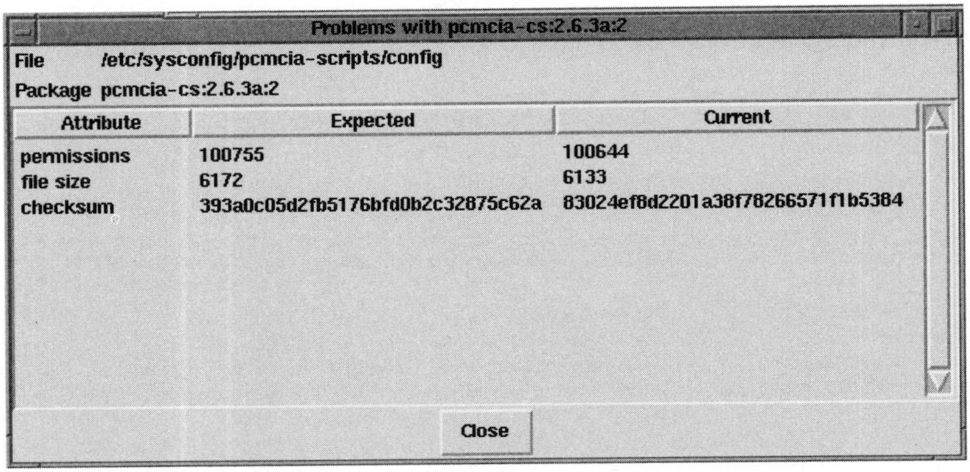

Problems with pcmcia-cs:2.6.3a:2
File /etc/sysconfig/pcmcia-scripts/config
Package pcmcia-cs:2.6.3a:2
Attribute
Expected
Current
permissions
100755
100644
file size
6172
6133
checksum
393a0c05d2fb5176bfd0b2c32875c62a
83024ef8d2201a38f78266571f1b5384
Close

Figure 9-8. Verification details

Installing New Packages

Installing new packages from glint is very simple. First look at the packages available for installation (see the section called "Viewing Available Packages" earlier in this chapter for details on how to do this). You may select any number of these (and query them if you're not sure what they are) for installation in the same manner you select packages for verification. If you want to install a single package or group, the context sensitive menus provide a shortcut for doing so. Figure 9-9 shows a window with some packages selected for installation.

After you've begun the installation, a window like the one in Figure 9-10 appears. It tracks the progress of the installation so you'll know something is happening. The top bar shows how much of the current package (whose name is listed inside of it) has been installed while the bottom graph shows how much of the total installation has been finished. The number of packages, package sizes, and time estimates are continually updated.

If a problem occurs during the installation, a window will appear listing any errors that occurred. If this happens, you should correct the problems and then try again.

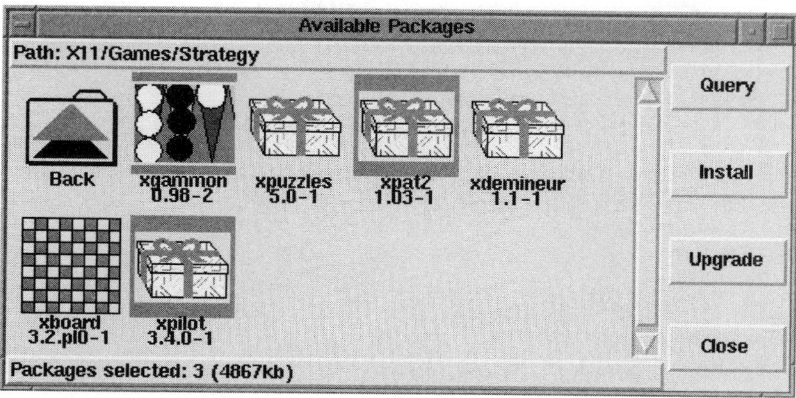

Figure 9-9. Packages selected for installation

Installing

	Total	Finished	Remaining
Packages	3	0	3
kbytes	4867	605	4262
Time	00:02:40	00:00:20	00:02:20

xpilot (1128kb)

Figure 9-10. Installation progress

After the installation has completed, the package and groups that have been installed are moved from the available window to the main glint window to show you that they have been successfully installed.

Upgrading packages

When a new version of a package has been released, it is easy to install it on your system. Select the packages from the window of available packages in the same way you select packages for installation. Both the `Upgrade` button and the context sensitive menus will begin the upgrade.

During the upgrade, you'll see a progress indicator like the one for installing packages. When it's finished, the installed packages will appear in the the main glint windows and any old versions of the packages will be removed.

It is much better to use the upgrade option than to uninstall the old versions of a package and then install the new one. Using upgrade ensures that any changes you made to package configuration files get preserved properly, while doing it manually could cause those changes to be lost.

If you run out of disk space during an installation, the install will fail. However, the package that was being installed when the error occurred may leave some files around. To clean this up, reinstall the package after you've made more disk space available.

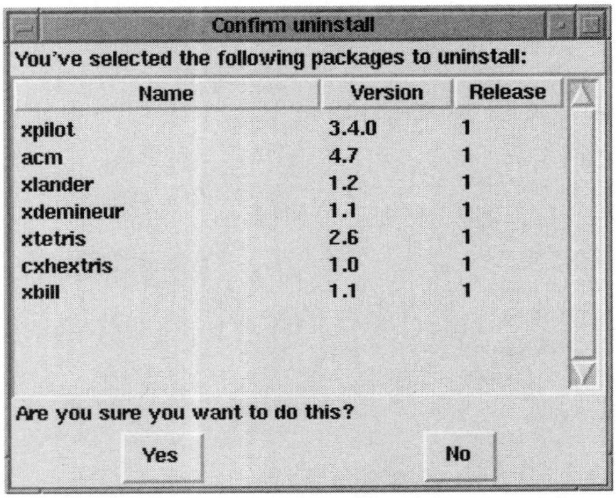

Confirm uninstall

You've selected the following packages to uninstall:

Name	Version	Release
xpilot	3.4.0	1
acm	4.7	1
xlander	1.2	1
xdemineur	1.1	1
xtetris	2.6	1
cxhextris	1.0	1
xbill	1.1	1

Are you sure you want to do this?

Yes   No

Figure 9–11. Uninstall window

Uninstalling Packages

Uninstalling a package is not the same as upgrading one. When a package is uninstalled, any files it uses that are not needed by other packages on your system get removed. Changed configuration files get copied to *filename*.`rpmsave` so you can reuse them later.

Like verifying and querying packages, you can remove a package through the buttons on the right of the glint window or through a context sensitive menu. Remember that when you make a choice from a group's menu, the operation gets performed an all of the packages in that group, so be careful!

Once you've begun the uninstall, glint asks for confirmation, showing a window like the one in Figure 9-11. All of the packages that are about to be uninstalled are listed. You should look at them all to ensure you're not about to remove something you want to keep. Clicking the `Yes` button will start the uninstallation process. After it completes, the packages and groups that have been removed will disappear from any windows they were in.

CHAPTER TEN

Frequently Asked Questions

This section will help you troubleshoot your system. It contains the answers to many common questions, and the solutions to many common problems. Please read it carefully before you ask something on the Net. A complete up–to–date version of the Red Hat FAQ is available at:

```
http://www.redhat.com/RedHat-FAQ
ftp://ftp.redhat.com/RedHat-FAQ
```

as well as by fingering or sending mail to *faq@redhat.com*.

If you ask something on the Net, and the answer is here or in the RedHat–FAQ, you'll waste everyone's time and you'll look silly.

General Questions

Where can I get information on Red Hat Linux?

There are many ways to get information on Red Hat products:

What	Where
General Information	*http://www.redhat.com* *ftp://ftp.redhat.com* email *info@redhat.com* *http://www.acc-corp.com* email *info@acc-corp.com*
Red Hat FAQ	*http://www.redhat.com/RedHat-FAQ* *ftp://ftp.redhat.com/RedHat-FAQ* email *faq@redhat.com*
Sales	(203) 454-5500 (800) 546-7274 (203) 454-2582 (fax)

What	Where
Sales, cont.	email *sales@redhat.com* *http://www.acc-corp.com* *http://www.redhat.com*

On what media is Red Hat Linux available?

It is available on CD-ROM and via FTP. Although a floppy installation is supported, as of this writing there are no companies selling Red Hat floppy disk sets.

The Red Hat FTP site is slow

There are several Red Hat Official mirrors of the Red Hat FTP site:

```
ftp://ftp.pht.com/pub/linux/redhat
ftp://sunsite.unc.edu/pub/Linux/distributions/redhat
ftp://sunsite.doc.ic.ac.uk/packages/linux/sunsite.unc-mirror/
                                    distributions/redhat
ftp://ftp.cms.uncwil.edu/linux/redhat
ftp://ftp.wilmington.net/linux/redhat
ftp://ftp.caldera.com/pub/mirrors/redhat
ftp://ftp.lasermoon.co.uk/pub/distributions/RedHat
ftp://ftp.cc.gatech.edu/pub/linux/distributions/redhat
ftp://uiarchive.cso.uiuc.edu/pub/systems/linux/distributions/
                                    redhat
ftp://ftp.ibp.fr/pub/linux/distributions/redhat
ftp://ftp.gwdg.de/pub/linux/install/redhat
ftp://ftp.uoknor.edu/linux/redhat
ftp://ftp.msu.ru/pub/Linux/RedHat
ftp://linux.ucs.indiana.edu/pub/linux/redhat
ftp://ftp.cvut.cz/pub/linux/redhat
ftp://ftp.ton.tut.fi/pub/Linux/RedHat
```

Any of these should provide you with a fast link to Red Hat upgrades or the entire distribution.

In the rest of this document, pathnames for Red Hat components are relative to the directories listed above for each mirror. Just concatenate that filename to any of the above mirror locations to find the file.

How do I get updates to RHCL as they happen?

Keep your eye on *current/updates/RPMS* on the mirrors, and subscribe to the *redhat–announce–list* mailing list.

Also check the *non–free* and *contrib* directories for packages that we can't distribute on CD-ROM and packages that users have contributed.

Are there any Red Hat mailing lists?

Yes! The mailing lists are very active with Red Hat users, and you will find that the folks on these lists are friendly and knowledgeable!

There are three mailing lists, and one digest.

redhat–list
: This list is for general discussion of Red Hat related issues.

redhat–digest
: This is a digest form of *redhat–list.* It gets the exact same postings, but they are concatenated so that you get 15 or 20 all in one email message. If you don't want to get up to 30 pieces of email per day from the *redhat–list,* you may want to subscribe to *redhat–digest.*

redhat–announce–list
: This list is limited to important announcements only, including new RPM packages, important security information, and other items that are too important for you to miss.

redhat–devel–list
: This list is for discussion of development issues related to Red Hat, including RPM, glint, the control–panel, and the installation process. If you want to contribute to Red Hat, this is the place to talk about it.

To subscribe to any of the above lists send email to *list–request@redhat.com* with the word "subscribe" in the subject line of the message.

To unsubscribe to any of the lists send email to *list–request@redhat.com* with the word "unsubscribe" in the subject line of the message.

How do I get support if I did not buy a Red Hat CD-ROM?

If you did not purchase Red Hat Linux from Red Hat Software, then you need to contact your vendor for support. If you got it for free off the Net, then you'll have to use the Net for support :–).

You may use the *redhat–list* mailing to discuss Red Hat related issues.

What's the quickest and best way to get support for RHCL?

The mailing lists are the best place to discuss Red Hat issues.

Something seems to be broken. How do I report it?

First, you should try to investigate and see if it really is a problem. You can use RPM to diagnose a number of simple problems. Read Chapter 6, *Package Management with RPM*, for some examples on how to use RPM to solve problems and find documentation.

Something seems to be missing. How do I report it?

Before reporting anything or sending mail to the mailing lists, you should first look around a little. Keep in mind that in all likelihood you do *not* have all the available rpms packages installed on your system.

On the mirrors, *current/RedHat/rpm–contents.gz* (or *RedHat/rpm–contents.gz* on your Red Hat CD–ROM) is a listing of all the files, in all the Red Hat RPM packages, along with descriptions. If you find yourself asking "Where is *rz*?" look there.

If you've really found a problem, send mail to *support@redhat.com*. Be as detailed as possible! For example, if you can't get Red Hat to see your SCSI drives, tell us:

- The kind of SCSI card you have
- The version of your kernel
- The SCSI IDs of your drives
- How many IDE drives you have
- Specific details of the problem

If your CD–ROM isn't recognized, tell us:

- The make and model of CD–ROM
- The type of interface (IDE, SB, etc.)
- The bootdisk version
- The hardware configuration

Again, be as detailed as possible about your problem.

What versions of Red Hat are there, and which do I have?

There have been several now. Here's a rundown of the versions and their release dates:

- Preview (or Beta), Summer '94
- Halloween, Fall '94

- Mother's Day 1.0, Summer '95
- Mother's Day 1.1; Late Summer '95
- Red Hat 2.0 Beta, Mid August '95
- Red Hat 2.0, September '95
- Red Hat 2.1, November '95

If you look at the *README* on your CD–ROM (or FTP site), it'll tell you what version of Red Hat you have.

What hardware is supported by Red Hat Linux?

We support all hardware that Linux supports on the Intel platform. Nothing more. For more information on hardware compatibility, see the Hardware–HOWTO at *ftp://sunsite.unc.edu/pub/Linux/docs/HOWTO/Hardware–HOWTO.*

Red Hat Software expects to have a *beta* version of Red Hat Linux for the Alpha available in early 1995.

I need more support. How can I get it?

You need the *Red Hat Support Program.* For more information, see *http://www.redhat.com.* It is basically a one–year subscription to Red Hat Linux and two hours of technical support via email, fax, or phone. We may also offer extra "deals" to Program members from time to time.

Contact Red Hat Software sales for ordering information at (800) 546–7274.

Does Red Hat Linux include source code?

Yes. We include the sources and build instructions (in the form of an RPM spec file and patches) for every single piece of Red Hat Linux. You can rebuild all of Red Hat with a single command (don't try this at home: *rpm —rebuild *.src.rpm*).

What version of the X Window System is included with Red Hat Linux?

Red Hat 2.1 is distributed with XFree86 3.1.2 and comes with a simple configuration tool (*Xconfigurator*). We have also installed third party X servers from Metrolink and X Inside with no problems.

What software packages do we ship in our latest release?

There are too many packages to list here. If you want the complete list, go to a Red Hat mirror and have a look in *current/RedHat/RPMS.* You can also browse all the RPM packages on the Red Hat web site, *http://www.redhat.com/rpms.* At our web site you can query each individual package to get the description and file list.

Installation Questions

A new Red Hat release just came out. Do I have to reinstall my system?

Absolutely not! If your system is working, you should never have to reinstall Red Hat Linux as a whole. All you need to do is replace individual packages or parts of the operating system when you want to upgrade, a task that RPM and glint make very easy.

I need to run the installation program again. How do I do it?

If you chose the wrong parameters by mistake when installing and your system is not working, or if you find that your partitions are set up wrong and you need to repartition the disk, you will have to reinstall everything.

If, on the other hand, you just want to install more software, mount additional partitions, or configure networking, use can use RPM and the control–panel to do this—without reinstalling your system.

Why am I missing some programs?

Try entering `df` at the shell prompt. If you have */* or */usr* showing up as 100% used, chances are your partitions were too small for the entire installation. Unfortunately, this does not result in any obvious error messages and you won't notice it unless you were watching the installation very closely (which most people don't when the thing tells you it is going to take 2 hours to install).

You will most likely need to reinstall and do one of two things: a) make your */* or */usr* partition larger or b) install fewer packages. If the express install filled up your system and you cannot make your partition bigger, you have two choices. You can do a step–by–step install and choose a fairly minimal setup, or don't let the Express Install choose your packages for you.

Do I need to reinstall if I didn't get a LILO prompt?

Not necessarily. You should be able to use the boot disk that you made for the install to boot to your root partition on the hard drive. Insert the disk, reboot the machine, and at the boot prompt, type:

```
linux ramdisk=0 root=/dev/xxxx
```

where *xxxx* is the hard drive and partition number. For instance, if you installed to the first partition of your first IDE drive, this would be hda1. If you installed to the third partition on your second drive, this would be hdb3. The second partition of your second SCSI drive would be sdb2.

If you don't remember what device name your root partition is, try what you *think* might work. The worst that will happen is that the kernel panics and halts. If this happens, reboot and try another partition.

Once you boot, you need to edit */etc/lilo.conf* and then run 'lilo'. For more information on how to do that properly, you need to mount your CD–ROM with Red Hat on it and install the *howto* package (if you haven't already installed it). You can then read the LILO–HOWTO in */usr/doc* to learn how to write a proper *lilo.conf*.

An example *lilo.conf* to boot Linux and DOS is below:

```
boot=/dev/hda
map=/boot/map
install=/boot/boot.b
prompt
timeout=50
image=/vmlinuz
        label=linux
        root=/dev/hdb2
        read-only
        append=""
other=/dev/hda1
        label = dos
```

You may also need a line in the `other` section with `table = /dev/hda` or whatever drive your DOS partition is on. The only lines from above that should change if you boot Linux and DOS are `boot`, `root`, and `other`. Some of what is there is optional, like the append and what you actually label the DOS partition (some people prefer msdos).

One caveat: make sure the `boot` line points to your first IDE drive, your first SCSI drive *if and only if* you have *no* IDE drives. That is the only place the machine looks to find LILO. You also need to be sure that the partition in the `boot` line is marked "Active" by either the DOS *fdisk*, or the Linux *fdisk* (or *cfdisk*). Here are the "rules" of where / must live:

- If you have 2 IDE drives, your root partition *must* live on one of them, *no matter what.* This also includes any IDE CD–ROM drives on your *primary* controller. If you have one IDE hard drive, and one IDE CD–ROM on the *primary* controller, you must install your root partition on the IDE hard drive.
- If you have 1 IDE drive and SCSI drives, your root partition *must* live on the IDE drive or the SCSI drive *that is at ID 0.* No other IDs will work.
- If you have SCSI only, your root partition *must* live on a drive at ID 0 or ID 1. No other IDs will work.

But I Want DOS to Boot by Default!

Easy. Just change the above */etc/lilo.conf* to:

```
boot=/dev/hda
map=/boot/map
install=/boot/boot.b
prompt
timeout=50
other=/dev/hda1
        label = dos
image=/vmlinuz
        label=linux
        root=/dev/hdb2
        read-only
        append = ""
```

and run `lilo` after saving the file.

How do I mount my CD-ROM?

If you installed from CD, you should be able to enter:

```
mount /mnt/cdrom
```

If you installed via NFS or FTP, you need to know what type of CD–ROM you have. The best way is to watch the boot messages as you reboot, or look at */var/adm/messages.* You most likely have an IDE CD–ROM that will show up as */dev/hdc* or */dev/hdd,* a Sound Blaster type CD–ROM that is */dev/sbpcd,* or a SCSI CD–ROM drive that is */dev/scd0.* In any case, you can enter the following:

```
mount -t iso9660 /dev/xxxx /mnt/cdrom
cd /mnt/cdrom
ls
```

substituting your device for */dev/xxxx*. You will be looking at the contents of the CD–ROM. You may want to add a line to your */etc/fstab* like:

```
/mnt/cdrom              /dev/xxxx        iso9660 ro,noauto
```

which will allow you to mount your CD–ROM by simply entering:

```
mount /mnt/cdrom
```

Why does my Trident 9400 show up as an 8900?

XFree86 3.1.1 currently doesn't support the advanced features of the 9400. The timing for the release of the 9400 was just bad for the release dates of 3.1.1, so they weren't able to add the support in. Now that the card is pretty popular and a new release of XFree86 is expected soon, we expect to see direct support in the next version of XFree86. For now, you can run resolutions all the way to 1024x768 at 60 hz. If you have trouble using Xconfigurator to set it up, you will probably find that xf86config will do the job (it just doesn't look as nice doing it).

Why does Linux see only part of my RAM?

There are a couple things that could be wrong. On *some* 386s, you need to compile your kernel with "Limit memory to 16M?" enabled. Some AMI BIOS motherboards have a memory option to split memory into two segments. You'll find it in your BIOS setup.

You may need to specify the amount of memory to the kernel at boot time from LILO. To try this, type: `linux mem=32M` at the lilo prompt. If that works, you can add `mem=32M` to the `append` line in your */etc/lilo.conf* and run `lilo`:

```
append = "mem=32M"
```

Don't forget to run `lilo` after editing the file.

Does Red Hat support the Adaptec 2940 SCSI Controller?

No, not directly. It is not supported in the current 1.2.x series of kernels, so we don't support it. We do have reports of it working, however. We also provide some experimental boot disks to help get it working. The boot disk images can be found on the mirrors in *current/images/2940* and *current/images/1332.*

Why can't I install to a partition greater than 9?

The install program had a bug in it, which is fixed in the current Red Hat 2.1 release. An updated root disk for Red Hat 2.0 is available from any mirror in *redhat–2.0/images*. Use it in place of your ramdisk2.img. *Do not do this if you have Red Hat 2.1! This problem is already fixed in 2.1.*

How do I install to my DOS partition?

You can't. No current Red Hat release supports UMSDOS installs. If you have one drive that has one big DOS partition with free space you want to use, you have two options. One is to back up all your DOS data somehow and then repartition the drive into smaller partitions and then restore the DOS data back to a DOS partition. You then have a free partition for Linux. The second choice is to use fips. Fips is a program that will let you change your partition size of a DOS partition without harming the data on it. It is *strongly* suggested that you back up your data before using fips. Red Hat Software makes no warranties or claims as to the suitability of using fips for this purpose nor does Red Hat guarantee that data will remain unharmed. I haven't heard of anyone having a bad experience with fips, but I won't guarantee it either.

Using Red Hat Linux

How do I get color ls to work?

Some of you may be accustomed to other distributions and the fact that color ls is installed by default. Red Hat Linux does not do that, but it is possible to set up. Simply put

```
eval 'dircolors'
```

in your */etc/profile* or *~/.bash_profile.* Of course, you need to ensure that the *color–ls* package is installed!

I rebuilt my kernel, but I got vmlinux instead of vmlinuz. Why?

You need to execute *make zImage* or *make zlilo* instead of just *make. make zlilo* is the best choice for most beginners as it will not only build the kernel, but also install it as the default for you if the make goes well. *make zImage* will build a compressed kernel and place it in *arch/i386/boot.* You must copy it to your root directory and run 'lilo' yourself to use this one.

If you used make, you got a file called *vmlinux.* This is an *uncompressed* kernel image, and will *not* work! LILO will only boot a compressed kernel.

Why are hostname resolutions taking so long?

Your name resolver may be looking at all the **.com** or **.edu** addresses. Edit your */etc/resolv.conf* and remove **com** and **edu** from your search path. This can be especially unsettling on a small network with a serial line to the Internet, and with a name server on the other side of the serial line. If you accidentally enter *telnet foO* when you meant *telnet foo*, you have to wait for it to search the entire **.com** hierarchy for *fo0.com* before it returns.

I compiled a program, but I can't run it. What gives?

Lets say you do the following as root:

```
gcc -o hello hello.c
hello
```

You'll get "`hello: command not found`"

Why?

By default, '.' is not in your path. You must run:

```
./hello
```

For security reasons, '.' should *not* in your path.

Why does iBCS break when I recompile my kernel?

You need to answer 'y' to the line that asks:

```
CONFIG_MODVERSIONS [n]
```

If you didn't do that, you'll need to rebuild your kernel and enable it. Also, if you are building a new version of the kernel, you'll need to install the iBCS source and rebuild that.

LICENSES

Nearly all of the software components on the Red Hat Linux CD–ROM are freely redistributable. A few of them require special permission to redistribute, and Red Hat Software, Inc. has obtained these permissions. The majority of the software components are distributable under the terms of one of the three licenses in this chapter. Please see each software component for precise distribution terms.

All the software on the CD–ROM produced by Red Hat Software is Copyright (C) 1995 by Red Hat Software, Inc. Unless otherwise noted, all such software is freely redistributable under the terms of the GNU Public License (GPL).

The terms Red Hat, RPM, and glint are trademarks of Red Hat Software, Inc.

The BSD Copyright

Copyright © 1991, 1992, 1993, 1994 The Regents of the University of California. All rights reserved.

Redistribution and use in source and binary forms, with or without modification, are permitted provided that the following conditions are met:

- Redistributions of source code must retain the above copyright notice, this list of conditions and the following disclaimer.
- Redistributions in binary form must reproduce the above copyright notice, this list of conditions and the following disclaimer in the documentation and/or other materials provided with the distribution.
- All advertising materials mentioning features or use of this software must display the following acknowledgement: This product includes software developed by the University of California, Berkeley and its contributors.

- Neither the name of the University nor the names of its contributors may be used to endorse or promote products derived from this software without specific prior written permission.

THIS SOFTWARE IS PROVIDED BY THE REGENTS AND CONTRIBUTORS "AS IS" AND ANY EXPRESS OR IMPLIED WARRANTIES, INCLUDING, BUT NOT LIMITED TO, THE IMPLIED WARRANTIES OF MERCHANTABILITY AND FITNESS FOR A PARTICULAR PURPOSE ARE DISCLAIMED. IN NO EVENT SHALL THE REGENTS OR CONTRIBUTORS BE LIABLE FOR ANY DIRECT, INDIRECT, INCIDENTAL, SPECIAL, EXEMPLARY, OR CONSEQUENTIAL DAMAGES (INCLUDING, BUT NOT LIMITED TO, PROCUREMENT OF SUBSTITUTE GOODS OR SERVICES; LOSS OF USE, DATA, OR PROFITS; OR BUSINESS INTERRUPTION) HOWEVER CAUSED AND ON ANY THEORY OF LIABILITY, WHETHER IN CONTRACT, STRICT LIABILITY, OR TORT (INCLUDING NEGLIGENCE OR OTHERWISE) ARISING IN ANY WAY OUT OF THE USE OF THIS SOFTWARE, EVEN IF ADVISED OF THE POSSIBILITY OF SUCH DAMAGE.

X Copyright

Copyright © 1987 X Consortium

Permission is hereby granted, free of charge, to any person obtaining a copy of this software and associated documentation files (the "Software"), to deal in the Software without restriction, including without limitation the rights to use, copy, modify, merge, publish, distribute, sublicense, and/or sell copies of the Software, and to permit persons to whom the Software is furnished to do so, subject to the following conditions:

The above copyright notice and this permission notice shall be included in all copies or substantial portions of the Software.

THE SOFTWARE IS PROVIDED "AS IS", WITHOUT WARRANTY OF ANY KIND, EXPRESS OR IMPLIED, INCLUDING BUT NOT LIMITED TO THE WARRANTIES OF MERCHANTABILITY, FITNESS FOR A PARTICULAR PURPOSE AND NONINFRINGEMENT. IN NO EVENT SHALL THE X CONSORTIUM BE LIABLE FOR ANY CLAIM, DAMAGES OR OTHER LIABILITY, WHETHER IN AN ACTION OF CONTRACT, TORT OR OTHERWISE, ARISING FROM, OUT OF OR IN CONNECTION WITH THE SOFTWARE OR THE USE OR OTHER DEALINGS IN THE SOFTWARE.

Except as contained in this notice, the name of the X Consortium shall not be used in advertising or otherwise to promote the sale, use, or other dealings in this Software without prior written authorization from the X Consortium.

Copyright © 1987 by Digital Equipment Corporation, Maynard, Massachusetts.

Permission to use, copy, modify, and distribute this software and its documentation for any purpose and without fee is hereby granted, provided that the above copyright notice appears in all copies and that both that copyright notice and this permission notice appear in supporting documentation, and that the name of Digital not be used in advertising or publicity pertaining to distribution of the software without specific, written prior permission.

DIGITAL DISCLAIMS ALL WARRANTIES WITH REGARD TO THIS SOFTWARE, INCLUDING ALL IMPLIED WARRANTIES OF MERCHANTABILITY AND FITNESS, IN NO EVENT SHALL DIGITAL BE LIABLE FOR ANY SPECIAL, INDIRECT OR CONSEQUENTIAL DAMAGES OR ANY DAMAGES WHATSOEVER RESULTING FROM LOSS OF USE, DATA OR PROFITS, WHETHER IN AN ACTION OF CONTRACT, NEGLIGENCE OR OTHER TORTIOUS ACTION, ARISING OUT OF OR IN CONNECTION WITH THE USE OR PERFORMANCE OF THIS SOFTWARE.

Gnu Public License

GNU GENERAL PUBLIC LICENSE Version 2, June 1991

Copyright (C) 1989, 1991 Free Software Foundation, Inc. 675 Massachusetts Avenue, Cambridge, MA 02139, USA Everyone is permitted to copy and distribute verbatim copies of this license document, but changing it is not allowed.

Preamble

The licenses for most software are designed to take away your freedom to share and change it. By contrast, the GNU General Public License is intended to guarantee your freedom to share and change free software—to make sure the software is free for all its users. This General Public License applies to most of the Free Software Foundation's software and to any other program whose authors commit to using it. (Some other Free Software Foundation software is covered by the GNU Library General Public License instead.) You can apply it to your programs, too.

When we speak of free software, we are referring to freedom, not price. Our General Public Licenses are designed to make sure that you have the freedom to distribute copies of free software (and charge for this service if you wish), that you receive source code or can get it if you want it, that you can change the software or use pieces of it in new free programs; and that you know you can do these things.

To protect your rights, we need to make restrictions that forbid anyone to deny you these rights or to ask you to surrender the rights. These restrictions translate to certain responsibilities for you if you distribute copies of the software, or if you modify it.

For example, if you distribute copies of such a program, whether gratis or for a fee, you must give the recipients all the rights that you have. You must make sure that they, too, receive or can get the source code. And you must show them these terms so they know their rights.

We protect your rights with two steps: (1) copyright the software, and (2) offer you this license which gives you legal permission to copy, distribute and/or modify the software.

Also, for each author's protection and ours, we want to make certain that everyone understands that there is no warranty for this free software. If the software is modified by someone else and passed on, we want its recipients to know that what they have is not the original, so that any problems introduced by others will not reflect on the original authors' reputations.

Finally, any free program is threatened constantly by software patents. We wish to avoid the danger that redistributors of a free program will individually obtain patent licenses, in effect making the program proprietary. To prevent this, we have made it clear that any patent must be licensed for everyone's free use or not licensed at all.

The precise terms and conditions for copying, distribution and modification follow.

GNU GENERAL PUBLIC LICENSE

TERMS AND CONDITIONS FOR COPYING, DISTRIBUTION AND MODIFICATION

0

This License applies to any program or other work that contains a notice placed by the copyright holder saying it may be distributed under the terms of this General Public License. The "Program," below, refers to any such program or work, and a "work based on the Program" means either the Program or any derivative work under copyright law: that is to say, a work containing the Program or a portion of it, either verbatim or with modifications and/or translated into another language. (Hereinafter, translation is included without limitation in the term "modification.") Each licensee is addressed as "you."

Activities other than copying, distribution, and modification are not covered by this License; they are outside its scope. The act of running the Program is not restricted, and the output from the Program is covered only if its contents constitute a work based on the Program (independent of having been made by running the Program). Whether that is true depends on what the Program does.

1

You may copy and distribute verbatim copies of the Program's source code as you receive it, in any medium, provided that you conspicuously and appropriately publish on each copy an appropriate copyright notice and disclaimer of warranty; keep intact all the notices that refer to this License and to the absence of any warranty; and give any other recipients of the Program a copy of this License along with the Program.

You may charge a fee for the physical act of transferring a copy, and you may at your option offer warranty protection in exchange for a fee.

2

You may modify your copy or copies of the Program or any portion of it, thus forming a work based on the Program, and copy and distribute such modifications or work under the terms of Section 1 above, provided that you also meet all of these conditions:

- You must cause the modified files to carry prominent noticesstating that you changed the files and the date of any change.
- You must cause any work that you distribute or publish, that inwhole or in part contains or is derived from the Program or any part thereof, to be licensed as a whole at no charge to all third parties under the terms of this License.
- If the modified program normally reads commands interactivelywhen run, you must cause it, when started running for such interactive use in the most ordinary way, to print or display an announcement including an appropriate copyright notice and a notice that there is no warranty (or else, saying that you provide a warranty) and that users may redistribute the program under these conditions, and telling the user how to view a copy of this License. (Exception: if the Program itself is interactive but does not normally print such an announcement, your work based on the Program is not required to print an announcement.)

These requirements apply to the modified work as a whole. If identifiable sections of that work are not derived from the Program, and can be reasonably considered independent and separate works in themselves, then this License, and its terms, do not apply to those sections when you distribute them as separate works. But when you distribute the same sections as part of a whole which is a work based on the Program, the distribution of the whole must be on the terms of this License, whose permissions for other licensees extend to the entire whole, and thus to each and every part regardless of who wrote it.

Thus, it is not the intent of this section to claim rights or contest your rights to work written entirely by you; rather, the intent is to exercise the right to control the distribution of derivative or collective works based on the Program.

In addition, mere aggregation of another work not based on the Program with the Program (or with a work based on the Program) on a volume of a storage or distribution medium does not bring the other work under the scope of this License.

3

You may copy and distribute the Program (or a work based on it, under Section 2) in object code or executable form under the terms of Sections 1 and 2 above provided that you also do one of the following:

- Accompany it with the complete corresponding machine readablesource code, which must be distributed under the terms of Sections 1 and 2 above on a medium customarily used for software interchange; or,
- Accompany it with a written offer, valid for at least threeyears, to give any third party, for a charge no more than your cost of physically performing source distribution, a complete machine–readable copy of the corresponding source code, to be distributed under the terms of Sections 1 and 2 above on a medium customarily used for software interchange; or,
- Accompany it with the information you received as to the offerto distribute corresponding source code. (This alternative is allowed only for noncommercial distribution and only if you received the program in object code or executable form with such an offer, in accord with Subsection b above.)

The source code for a work means the preferred form of the work for making modifications to it. For an executable work, complete source code means all the source code for all modules it contains, plus any associated interface definition files, plus the scripts used to control compilation and installation of the executable. However, as a special exception, the source code distributed need not include anything that is normally distributed (in either source or binary form) with the major components (compiler, kernel, and so on) of the operating system on which the executable runs, unless that component itself accompanies the executable.

If distribution of executable or object code is made by offering access to copy from a designated place, then offering equivalent access to copy the source code from the same place counts as distribution of the source code, even though third parties are not compelled to copy the source along with the object code.

4

You may not copy, modify, sublicense, or distribute the Program except as expressly provided under this License. Any attempt otherwise to copy, modify, sublicense or distribute the Program is void, and will automatically terminate your rights under this License. However, parties who have received copies, or rights, from you under this License will not have their licenses terminated so long as such parties remain in full compliance.

5

You are not required to accept this License, since you have not signed it. However, nothing else grants you permission to modify or distribute the Program or its derivative works. These actions are prohibited by law if you do not accept this License. Therefore, by modifying or distributing the Program (or any work based on the Program), you indicate your acceptance of this License to do so, and all its terms and conditions for copying, distributing or modifying the Program or works based on it.

6

Each time you redistribute the Program (or any work based on the Program), the recipient automatically receives a license from the original licensor to copy, distribute or modify the Program subject to these terms and conditions. You may not impose any further restrictions on the recipients' exercise of the rights granted herein. You are not responsible for enforcing compliance by third parties to this License.

7

If, as a consequence of a court judgment or allegation of patent infringement or for any other reason (not limited to patent issues), conditions are imposed on you (whether by court order, agreement or otherwise) that contradict the conditions of this License, they do not excuse you from the conditions of this License. If you cannot distribute so as to satisfy simultaneously your obligations under this License and any other pertinent obligations, then as a consequence you may not distribute the Program at all. For example, if a patent license would not permit royalty–free redistribution of the Program by all those who receive copies directly or indirectly through you, then the only way you could satisfy both it and this License would be to refrain entirely from distribution of the Program.

If any portion of this section is held invalid or unenforceable under any particular circumstance, the balance of the section is intended to apply and the section as a whole is intended to apply in other circumstances.

It is not the purpose of this section to induce you to infringe any patents or other property right claims or to contest validity of any such claims; this section has the sole purpose of protecting the integrity of the free software distribution system, which is implemented by public license practices. Many people have made generous contributions to the wide range of software distributed through that system in reliance on consistent application of that system; it is up to the author/donor to decide if he or she is willing to distribute software through any other system and a licensee cannot impose that choice.

This section is intended to make thoroughly clear what is believed to be a consequence of the rest of this License.

8

If the distribution and/or use of the Program is restricted in certain countries either by patents or by copyrighted interfaces, the original copyright holder who places the Program under this License may add an explicit geographical distribution limitation excluding those countries, so that distribution is permitted only in or among countries not thus excluded. In such case, this License incorporates the limitation as if written in the body of this License.

9

The Free Software Foundation may publish revised and/or new versions of the General Public License from time to time. Such new versions will be similar in spirit to the present version, but may differ in detail to address new problems or concerns.

Each version is given a distinguishing version number. If the Program specifies a version number of this License which applies to it and "any later version", you have the option of following the terms and conditions either of that version or of any later version published by the Free Software Foundation. If the Program does not specify a version number of this License, you may choose any version ever published by the Free Software Foundation.

10

If you wish to incorporate parts of the Program into other free programs whose distribution conditions are different, write to the author to ask for permission. For software which is copyrighted by the Free Software Foundation, write to the Free Software Foundation; we sometimes make exceptions for this. Our decision will be guided by the two goals of preserving the free status of all derivatives of our free software and of promoting the sharing and reuse of software generally.

11

BECAUSE THE PROGRAM IS LICENSED FREE OF CHARGE, THERE IS NO WARRANTY FOR THE PROGRAM, TO THE EXTENT PERMITTED BY APPLICABLE LAW. EXCEPT WHEN OTHERWISE STATED IN WRITING THE COPYRIGHT HOLDERS AND/OR OTHER PARTIES PROVIDE THE PROGRAM "AS IS" WITHOUT WARRANTY OF ANY KIND, EITHER EXPRESSED OR IMPLIED, INCLUDING, BUT NOT LIMITED TO, THE IMPLIED WARRANTIES OF MERCHANTABILITY AND FITNESS FOR A PARTICULAR PURPOSE. THE ENTIRE RISK AS TO THE QUALITY AND PERFORMANCE OF THE PROGRAM IS WITH YOU. SHOULD THE PROGRAM PROVE DEFECTIVE, YOU ASSUME THE COST OF ALL NECESSARY SERVICING, REPAIR OR CORRECTION.

IN NO EVENT UNLESS REQUIRED BY APPLICABLE LAW OR AGREED TO IN WRITING WILL ANY COPYRIGHT HOLDER, OR ANY OTHER PARTY WHO MAY

MODIFY AND/OR REDISTRIBUTE THE PROGRAM AS PERMITTED ABOVE, BE LIABLE TO YOU FOR DAMAGES, INCLUDING ANY GENERAL, SPECIAL, INCIDENTAL OR CONSEQUENTIAL DAMAGES ARISING OUT OF THE USE OR INABILITY TO USE THE PROGRAM (INCLUDING BUT NOT LIMITED TO LOSS OF DATA OR DATA BEING RENDERED INACCURATE OR LOSSES SUSTAINED BY YOU OR THIRD PARTIES OR A FAILURE OF THE PROGRAM TO OPERATE WITH ANY OTHER PROGRAMS), EVEN IF SUCH HOLDER OR OTHER PARTY HAS BEEN ADVISED OF THE POSSIBILITY OF SUCH DAMAGES.

Appendix

How to Apply These Terms to Your New Programs

If you develop a new program, and you want it to be of the greatest possible use to the public, the best way to achieve this is to make it free software which everyone can redistribute and change under these terms.

To do so, attach the following notices to the program. It is safest to attach them to the start of each source file to most effectively convey the exclusion of warranty; and each file should have at least the "copyright" line and a pointer to where the full notice is found.

```
$<$one line to give the program's name and a brief idea of what it does.$>$
Copyright (C) 19yy  $<$name of author$>$
This program is free software; you can redistribute it and/or modify
it under the terms of the GNU General Public License as published by
the Free Software Foundation; either version 2 of the License, or
(at your option) any later version.
This program is distributed in the hope that it will be useful,
but WITHOUT ANY WARRANTY; without even the implied warranty of
MERCHANTABILITY or FITNESS FOR A PARTICULAR PURPOSE. See the
GNU General Public License for more details.
You should have received a copy of the GNU General Public License
along with this program; if not, write to the Free Software
Foundation, Inc., 675 Mass Ave, Cambridge, MA 02139, USA.
```

Also add information on how to contact you by electronic and paper mail.

If the program is interactive, make it output a short notice like this when it starts in an interactive mode:

```
Gnomovision version 69, Copyright © 19yy name of author
Gnomovision comes with ABSOLUTELY NO WARRANTY; for details type 'show w'.
This is free software, and you are welcome to redistribute it
under certain conditions; type 'show c' for details.
```

The hypothetical commands 'show w' and 'show c' should show the appropriate parts of the General Public License. Of course, the commands you use may be called something other than 'show w' and 'show c'; they could even be mouse–clicks or menu items—whatever suits your program.

You should also get your employer (if you work as a programmer) or your school, if any, to sign a "copyright disclaimer" for the program, if necessary. Here is a sample; alter the names:

```
Yoyodyne, Inc., hereby disclaims all copyright interest in the program
'Gnomovision' (which makes passes at compilers) written by James Hacker.
$<$signature of Ty Coon$>$, 1 April 1989
Ty Coon, President of Vice
```

This General Public License does not permit incorporating your program into proprietary programs. If your program is a subroutine library, you may consider it more useful to permit linking proprietary applications with the library. If this is what you want to do, use the GNU Library General Public License instead of this License.

Linux Library CD

This Documentation CD, compiled by Eric Troan of Red Hat Software, which features a superfast browser, is a massive compilation of available documentation, on Linux and related technologies.

Featuring the equivalent of over 40,000 pages of fully searchable documentation this is the tool you need to save time and frustration in trying to find answers to your most obscure questions about Linux.

Use Red Hat's Linux Library CD to:

Quickly Find Answers: All the available references to any question about Linux, the X Window System, the Compilers, etc. that has ever been written and made available on the Internet archives.

Run Linux with Less Effort: Quick access to the answers you need, when you need them will allow you to solve your Linux installation configuration, and questions faster than ever.

Learn UNIX: You get all the reference material you need for learning C, C++, and other compilers, the X Window System with window managers, full UNIX networking including TCP/IP, SLIP and PPP, Sendmail, email, and more.

Advanced Uses: Research for writing manuals for Linux products. Updates on the progress of these technologies.

What You Get:

- **Browser Application**: A high-speed X Window-based search engine behind an elegant graphical browser that makes searching this material fast and easy.
- **Complete works of the Linux Documentation Project**, including all texts and how-to's
- **Linux and Linux-related man pages**: System Admin, Security and Privacy, JPEG and MPEG, lists of free software, etc.
- **10,000+ Pages of Content**: In short, you get everything, but here is a partial list:
  - **Internet Engineering RFCs**
  - **Complete comp.os.linux.announce archive**
  - **GNU docs**.
  - **Usenet FAQs** on language compilers for Linux
  - **And much more**

Only $39.95 from Red Hat Software

tel: (800) 454-5502 or (203) 454-5500 • fax: (203) 454-2582
email: *info@redhat.com* • *http: //www.redhat.com*

Red Hat's ACC Linux Catalog

This is the leading catalog of Linux distrbutions and applications. Whether you need Motif for your graphical application projects or professional quality databases, spreadsheets, or development environments, this catalog is for you.

Just fill out the form below, and fax, email, or call Red Hat Software's ACC Catalog to reserve your copy today.

Name: . . . .

Company: . . . .

Apt/Suite/Mail Stop: . . . .

Street: . . . .

City: . . . . .State: . . . . .Zip: . . . .

Country: . . . .

Phone: . . . . .Fax: . . . . .Email: . . . .

tel: (800) 454-5502 or (203) 454-5500 • fax: (203) 454-2582
email: *info@acc-corp.com* • *http: //www.redhat.com*

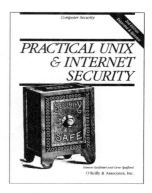

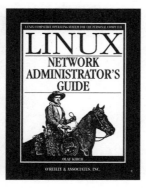